"Becky and her husband, Dick, ha  ix
continents, including seven years d
to be the most secular region of t l
insight have been distilled in *Stay* s
for encouraging faithful evangelis
the case, and distribute it as far as y. Buy it by

D.A. Carson, Founder, The Gospel Coalition

"In this generation, no other writer, teacher, scholar, or preacher has a firmer grasp on the power of evangelism than Rebecca Manley Pippert. And no one does a better job of communicating the joys and challenges of disciple-making. Her stories and examples are compelling."

Liz Curtis Higgs, Author, *Bad Girls of the Bible* and *Thorn in My Heart*

"Fresh, natural, straightforward—Becky Pippert may be one of the most gifted and fruitful communicators today, but she makes evangelism what it should be: the best news ever, for all who know it to share with all who don't."

Os Guinness, Author, *The Call*

"I was so thrilled by this book. Time and again I was shown how the great truths about God can be used to equip the church for evangelism. From now on, as I train churches, I'm going to be standing on Becky's shoulders."

Rico Tice, Founder, Christianity Explored Ministries;
Author, *Honest Evangelism*

"From the opening pages, I knew this would be a book worth reading, not only because the subject matter is so important but also because the writing style of its author is so engaging—practical, winsome, and gracious."

Glenn Davies, Archbishop of Sydney, Australia

"As you journey through these pages your mind and your heart will be gripped by the beauty, clarity, and power of the good news. Don't be surprised if you experience a wonderful sense of confidence to share this news with the world, starting with your neighbor."

Crawford Loritts, Pastor; Radio Host; Author

"Here is a book that mixes realism, freshness, gospel engagement and the pragmatic wisdom of someone who has "lived it," and it's all rooted in a strong biblical gospel base. *Stay Salt* should be a staple for any church bookstall, though copies won't stay there for very long!"

Hugh Palmer, Rector, All Souls Langham Place, London

"Not just inspirational and heartwarming, this book will renew your sense of both the wonder of the gospel and the privilege of sharing it."

Lindsay Brown, International Director, The Lausanne Movement

"Becky's training of thousands of UCCF students and staff kick-started some of the most fruitful personal and small-group evangelism we have ever experienced in British universities. Her genius seems to be the ability to excel in multiple areas simultaneously—*Stay Salt* blends theological precision with humour and vulnerability, and combines the urgency and priority of evangelism with God's interest in the whole person. Surely a must-read for the whole church."

Richard Cunningham, Director of UCCF: The Christian Unions

"No one has done more over the years to help me understand—and taste— the saltiness of the gospel than Becky. *Stay Salt* underscores just how powerfully and urgently we need to live and share this good news."

Mark Labberton, President, Fuller Theological Seminary, California

"Pippert grips us by the throat with the urgency of the gospel and leads us by the hand as we wonder how we might share it more often. This book will shake you. But it won't tear you down. With stories of fear and failure, as well as those of joyful fruit, Pippert inspires us to speak the truth in love to friends and strangers, be they university lecturers or hair stylists."

Rebecca McLaughlin, Author, *Confronting Christianity*

"*Out of the Saltshaker* was one of the most important books on evangelism written over the last generation. *Stay Salt* may be the best book on witness for the next generation. I don't know of a more lucid or penetrating book on evangelism to put into the hands of a Christian."

Timothy Keller, Founding Pastor Emeritus, Redeemer Presbyterian Church, Manhattan

"How refreshing to read a book on evangelism that presents the gospel in a way that is refreshingly biblical, joyfully inspiring, and powerfully relevant."

Ajith Fernando, Teaching Director, Youth for Christ, Sri Lanka

"Joyfully summons us into the new and sometimes daunting landscape of a post-Christian world with practical advice and insights."

Timothy Tennent, President, Asbury Theological Seminary, Kentucky

"*Stay Salt* has been written for today's people, and squarely faces today's conditions and prevailing secularism. Becky's enthusiasm, positive attitude, and refusal to be dismayed are infectious. A must-read for everyone!"

Benjamin Kwashi, Archbishop of Jos, Nigeria

"This is brilliant. Pippert guides us on how to tell people about Jesus in a culture that can seem impenetrable to the gospel. This book contains a contagious passion for the gospel, a perceptive wisdom about the world we live in, a profound understanding of God, and a deep practicality."

J.John, Evangelist and Author

REBECCA
MANLEY PIPPERT

STAY
SALT

Becky Pippert
MINISTRIES

www.beckypippert.org

Stay Salt
© Rebecca Manley Pippert, 2020

Published by:
The Good Book Company

thegoodbook.com | www.thegoodbook.co.uk
thegoodbook.com.au | thegoodbook.co.nz | thegoodbook.co.in

Published in association with the literary agency of Wolgemuth & Associates.

Unless indicated, all Scripture references are taken from the Holy Bible, New International Version. Copyright © 2011 Biblica, Inc.™ Used by permission.

ISBN: 9781784984366 | Printed in Denmark

Design by André Parker

This book is dedicated in grateful memory
of my beloved mother, Sue Manley:
February 21, 1930 – August 28, 2019

And to my husband, Dick: my partner,
my protector, and my joy, whom I love in
a place where there's no space or time.

CONTENTS

FOREWORD

by Ravi Zacharias

Two millennia ago, the evangelist chosen by God and set apart for evangelism and instruction was the apostle Paul. When you read his writings, you sense a person who was profoundly committed to proclaiming the good news of Jesus Christ, and who combined the rare strengths of theological integrity and methodological relevance. The message and the means must always be in keeping with each other.

In our time, few have done more to promote these twin realities than Becky Pippert, in her writings and her speaking. Two generations ago, her book *Out of the Saltshaker* captured the hearts and the imagination of wide audiences, and helped make them the salt of the earth. I have had the privilege of teaming up with Becky at home and around the world, and I have watched her impact. Now *Stay Salt* provides a brilliant, holistic approach: one of "being" and "doing" and "telling" the good news of the gospel.

The story is told of a man who served in George Washington's cabinet. He was totally bald. The top of his head would have been the envy of a shiny billiard ball. But in contrast to that barren scalp, he had a long, flowing bushy beard. Washington pointed to him, with a touch of humor, as someone particularly reflective of the problem of "overproduction and poor distribution."

That may well be the problem that we, as Christians, have lived with in terms of evangelism for the past two generations. Even more do I notice this problem of "overproduction and poor distribution" as I meet and talk with the next generation. We are not doing too well at being "out there" and sharing our lives and our message with the people God has placed in our neighborhoods, our workplaces, our friendship groups, and so on.

Sometimes I fear that we don't really understand either the lost or the message of "being found." Our Lord spoke of himself as being like a shepherd who left ninety-nine sheep in the fold to go looking for the one lost one (Luke 15 v 3-7). To be sure, it doesn't mean that he left the ninety-nine unprotected. But he did go looking. Sadly, in our times, sometimes the ninety-nine are unfed and the lost one is unpursued.

Becky, with her passion and her keen understanding of our restless times, brings a combination of the simple and the sublime to the message we need and must share—a combination that we need now more than ever. Whether our reticence stems from being untaught or being fearful, she approaches this challenge to make a difference in every reader.

Stay Salt contains three critical sections: Becky helps us understand how our fears in evangelism are met by God providing his supernatural "Means." In the section on the "Message," we learn the depth and beauty of the gospel, and (of special importance) Becky shows us how to help skeptics see the gospel's relevance and beauty for them. Then in the "Model" section, we see how Jesus' way of witnessing can resonate so beautifully with our present culture. All of this, coupled with powerful stories and illustrations, will help everyone, including non-evangelists, to be effective witnesses for such a time as this.

I remember that when I first started doing evangelistic preaching, a good message would bring a great turnout to hear what that message was. Sadly, the corruption of substance and obvious errors in forms have left the evangelist oftentimes without an audience. People have made a caricature of the message and mocked our methods. Today a tepid Christianity is set beside a scorching paganism. So many of us simply have no idea how beautiful the message is and how powerful the truth is.

Becky's passion is for all of us to start or keep sharing that beautiful truth. Her spirit is contagious, and her writing is inspiring. I commend Becky's desire to light new fires in our hearts so that we would go to meet people where they are, rather than waiting for them to come where we are: in other words, that we would stay salt. For salt is what is needed in an insipid and bored culture. Spreading the taste of the gospel is what it will take to bring the delight of what life was intended to be.

In closing, a little illustration will help. A few weeks ago, for the first time, I had all of my grandchildren in the audience at a rather large gathering. At the end of the meeting, two comments were incredibly instructive. My six-year-old granddaughter said as she was leaving, "That was quite a show." It took her parents a few moments to realize that she had "participated" in the event by consuming everything through the medium of a giant screen. For her, it was a "show" that she came to see, and it had much in common with all other shows. Our four-year-old grandchild had a different take and complained, "Pappa didn't look at me even once."

There you have it. The size of the audience made the means look like a show. For the same reason, it made it appear impersonal.

Stay Salt rescues us from both those dangers by showing what loving, compelling, personal and authentic witnessing looks like. We have an impact to make and a personal connection to make as we present the gospel message. Few do this as well as the author of this book. You will be a better witness for our Lord by taking these truths to heart. This is a timely book of timeless truth.

Ravi Zacharias
Speaker and Author

INTRODUCTION

The one thing that unites all Christians, now and throughout history, is our joyful assurance that the greatest thing that ever happened on our planet is the birth, death, resurrection, and ascension of Jesus Christ. The message of the gospel is quite simply the best news ever!

So here is my question: if this is so, why do so many Christians struggle to share the glorious news of the gospel? How can we believe that there is no greater news in the world but still feel unable or unwilling to tell others?

My husband, Dick, and I have long been engaged in evangelism ministry in America and around the world. We have worked in every continent, and recently we lived in Europe—parts of which are considered to be among the most secular places on earth—for seven years.

Two years ago, we returned to live in America, and I was interviewed on a national radio show which included a phone-in Q&A session. The producer said before my interview, "Becky, I know you and your husband have done evangelism ministry all over the world, and that recently you have lived and ministered in Europe. You need to know that things have changed in America. To be honest, American Christians are far more interested in living the gospel and demonstrating their witness by serving the needy and caring for their cities than they are in any verbal expression of faith. To be very honest, I think the light has gone out for that kind of evangelism. So don't worry if no one phones in."

What happened after my interview? All the phones lit up as people called in from across the country!

The callers' comments were very revealing. Every caller spoke of someone they cared deeply about who was not a Christian, but they felt fearful about engaging in a spiritual discussion with them. They said they longed for their friends to come to Christ, but because they felt inadequate in talking about faith, they were praying that another Christian would do it for them. All their fears were similar: *How do I raise the topic of faith naturally? What if I offend them or they reject me? What if they raise questions that I can't answer?* Nearly everyone said they wished their churches would help train them in evangelism—not in a formulaic, memorized, one-size-fits-all approach, but in the way that I had been describing in the interview.

One thing has become clear to me: never has there been a greater need to share Christ with the world, starting with our own neighbor—and never have believers felt more ill-equipped.

Why are Christians, especially in the West, struggling to share their faith? While in most parts of the world Christianity is growing dramatically, this is not the case in the West. Europe and Canada are secular—post-Christian. Statistics suggest that America is moving decidedly in the same direction. Influential voices are increasingly hostile and antagonistic to true Christian faith. The major currents shaping our culture present real challenges for the gospel: the collapse of absolute truth; the shift from objective authority to personal preference; the "designer religion" approach of picking and choosing what we believe, cafeteria style; the sexual revolution... The list goes on.

Some Christians feel angry about this.

Some Christians feel intimidated by this.

Some Christians feel defeated by this.

I feel hopeful.

Because while we are living in challenging times for the gospel, we are also living in remarkable times that are full of opportunities for the gospel. As my friend, the social critic and author Os Guinness, has written:

> "Our age is quite simply the greatest opportunity for Christian witness since the time of Jesus and the apostles, and our response should be to seize the opportunity with bold and imaginative enterprise. If ever the 'wide and effective door' that St. Paul wrote of has been reopened for the gospel, it is now."
>
> (*Fool's Talk*, page 16)

FRUIT FROM BURNED-OVER GROUND

Without question, the landscape in the West has changed considerably since I wrote my first book on evangelism, *Out of the Saltshaker*, in 1979. Back then it was a fairly radical idea to call Christians to an incarnational approach to witness, to challenge them to get out of the saltshaker and into the world: that is, to encourage them not to live in a Christian bubble but to genuinely befriend unbelievers, and to share the gospel as part of a relationship rather than using a hit-and-run approach.

Now, 40 years later, I am writing my second book on evangelism— because we need to learn again to share our faith in a confident, compassionate, compelling way in this new, post-Christian world. I remember when we were planning to move to Europe, and some well-meaning friends of ours counseled against it:

"It's burned-over ground for the gospel, Becky."

It wasn't. The secularized soil of Europe proved very fertile for the gospel. The fruit was tremendous. And this book is really the result of the lessons we learned.

What we have seen in our ministry is that even as our cultural landscape becomes increasingly secular, secularism does not have the power to erase our human longings for meaning and worth. If anything, it increases them. God has placed a longing for identity, meaning, and purpose in all human hearts; so, even if people can't quite articulate what they feel they are missing, the longing and wistfulness are there. But they will not know where to look unless Christians both live and tell the good news of what God has done for all in Christ.

REACH IN

When we returned to live in America, I found myself increasingly identifying with Lesslie Newbigin, the late British theologian, author and missionary. After years of living abroad in India, Newbigin returned to his home in England and was shocked by two things: first, the level of the secularization of England; and second, the impact that the secular culture was having on Christians.

He realized that the challenge wasn't only how to reach unbelievers with the gospel, but how to reach believers with the gospel as well! And that is, I believe, the challenge for all Christians everywhere. In the West the challenge comes from living in a post-truth, post-Christian culture that reflects the distortions of post-modernity.[1] This means we need to deepen our love for Jesus and to discover him with fresh eyes: to allow the truth of the gospel to have its full effect in us and to find effective ways to communicate the gospel for such a time as this.

Our problem, however, is that we have been far more influenced by secular culture than we realize. We are in great danger of believing the gospel in our heads, while functioning like skeptics because we have adopted a more secular view of reality, without recognizing it. We need to recover our confidence that the gospel is truly relevant to secular people today—that God and his gospel still retain the power to change lives. We need to see why we should be involved in evangelism even if we don't feel gifted at it. We need to remember why it is worth putting ourselves in situations where we could be rejected.

If we are going to reach out with the gospel, we also need to reach *in* with the gospel: into our own hearts and minds. This is our double challenge. To be credible messengers of our incredible gospel message we have to understand and truly believe the gospel ourselves! Our emphasis must never be on numbers or techniques, formulas or manipulation, but on authenticity,

---

1 While much of the emphasis of the book is about dealing with the challenges we face in the secular West, Dick and I have spent significant time ministering in the Global South, where our brothers and sisters have taught us so much. This book will also be relevant even in the countries where evangelism is flourishing, for three reasons: first, because Christian leaders in the Global South speak of their need for a deeper understanding of discipleship and the gospel; second, because even with our deep cultural differences, it is still our common humanity that unites us; and third, because the challenges we face in the West will offer insight and understanding if one day "our" struggles become "your" struggles—struggles which seem to be emerging already in the larger cities of the Global South.

credibility, and spiritual power. And so this book aims to excite us about the depth and beauty of the gospel, even as it equips us to share that gospel.

As we've spoken to and listened to countless thousands of Christians right around the world, helping them to both understand the gospel and to share it winsomely, we've often heard three heartfelt reasons why they are struggling or why they choose to remain quiet. Those three reasons provide the structure for this book.

We Feel Inadequate

We continually hear of the deep sense of inadequacy that Christians have about sharing their faith. They wonder how God could possibly use them in this current era. This is another way of saying that they fear that God may not come through. In other words, they are struggling with pockets of unbelief. They also suspect that evangelism is a specialized call and not for people like themselves. While they don't realize it, what they are really saying is that evangelism is up to them alone, and that is why they panic.

So we'll begin this book looking at the *Means* for witness. We'll see that God has given us all the divine resources we need for life and for witness—that the key is not whether we are great evangelists but realizing that God has empowered all of us through his Spirit to be his witnesses. Accepting our limitations and enjoying our limitless God is a game-changer not only in our walk with Christ but also in our witness.

We Think We Don't Know Enough

Another area of insecurity in Christians is feeling that they lack knowledge. They fear they do not understand the gospel well enough to explain it or defend it. They don't know how to answer the questions that skeptics will raise. Nor do they know how to help non-Christians see the beauty and relevance of the gospel to their lives.

That is why the second section is on the *Message*. We'll look carefully at each aspect of the gospel: creation, the fall, the cross, the resurrection, and Christ's return. We will remind ourselves of what each aspect of the gospel means and why it's so wonderful. We'll look at the pushback we'll receive from skeptics and some possible ways to answer their questions. And, crucially, we'll see how we can use each part of the gospel message to connect with the concerns and priorities that both seekers and skeptics have, and in ways that show the beauty and the relevance of the gospel.

We Lack Confidence

What we hear repeatedly is "I am just not sure how to do this. I really do want to share my faith—but I don't know where to start." So our last section is focused on the *Model*: what we can learn from Jesus and the early church about the "how" of witness. We'll explore how we can effectively share the gospel with both people who are spiritually open and those who are spiritually closed.

The purpose of this book is to help us to rise to the challenge of our time: speaking for our Lord in a way that reflects the wonder of who God is; communicating the beauty, depth, and relevance of the gospel that he has entrusted to us; becoming Spirit-dependent so that, through God's Spirit, we may be able to penetrate the resistance and stubbornness of minds and hearts that do not yet believe—in short, to help us find effective ways to share our faith even with—especially with—all the challenges that today's world presents.

Are Christians ready for this new age? Can we really communicate the gospel effectively? I emphatically say "Yes!" Because though our context and culture have changed, the power of the gospel has not. The riches and the resources that God has given to all Christians are still the same. Our task is learning how to apply all that we have received from God so that we can witness to the truth about him in ways that are effective and that truly connect with people today. We do not need to get angry, shouting at our culture. We do not need to feel defeated, staying silent in our culture. We can be hopeful, as we share the message that the whole word so desperately needs to hear. To put it another way, we can still be disciple-makers. We can—we must—stay salt!

SECTION ONE:
THE MEANS

CHAPTER ONE

SHUT DOWN
ON CAMPUS

I am not a "cradle Christian." In fact, for a long time I wasn't a Christian at all.

For several years I would have described myself as a wistful agnostic. I sensed something was missing: I had a longing I couldn't name, a thirst I couldn't fill, an ache for something I couldn't quite put my finger on.

I recently discovered a file of papers that I had written for an English class in my final year as a high-school student. I was astonished to see how clearly the papers revealed my search for meaning. In one paper I wrote, "What the author addresses in this novel I identify with as well. Does this nostalgia—this sense that we are created for something more—that something more seems promised—have any answer in objective reality? Is there an answer to this 'inconsolable thirst' that he writes about?"

The high school I attended was a public school, not a Christian one; nevertheless my teacher wrote on the margin side, "Becky, you are on the most important journey any human being can ever travel. Though you may not know it, you are searching for God. Do not settle for cheap substitutes. Knock on every door and keep knocking until you have your answer. Whatever you do, don't give up!"

In my search for meaning I explored other religions and other philosophies. Everything I read left me unsatisfied. Yet I had never investigated Christianity, nor read one page of the Bible, because I assumed that, having been raised in North America, I already understood it.

Then I read two books that changed my life. The first was the novel, *The Fall*, by Albert Camus, a French atheist existential-ist, who convinced me that I was a sinner. That may sound an odd conclusion to draw from reading an atheist author, but his unflinching analysis of the human heart was so devastating that it erased any hope of my ever becoming an optimistic humanist who saw only the bright side of human nature. My trouble with Camus, however, was that while he was deeply realistic about the dark side of human nature, he had no satisfactory answers to explain the good that we do see.

I then came across a book by C.S. Lewis, *Mere Christianity*. Lewis introduced me to the landscape of Christianity. While there were superficial similarities among the major religions, I was struck by how different the Christian faith was from any-thing I had read. Lewis also sparked my interest in the Bible. I began reading the Gospels and found myself captivated by Jesus. Ultimately I surrendered and committed my life to Jesus Christ—a story I'll talk more about in the next chapter.

FINDING THE HUNGER

Shortly after I became a Christian, I went away to university. I was a young Christian with very little Bible knowledge, but I knew that Christians were supposed to tell others about Jesus.

The problem was that I lacked the courage. Like many Christians I meet today, I assumed, sharing my faith meant proclaiming the message to every person I met, without drawing breath. I hadn't a clue about how to raise the topic of faith naturally. I worried that I'd offend people and that I wouldn't be able to answer their questions. So I remained silent, hoping people would somehow catch on by seeing my life.

In my first year at university I had two very significant experiences. First, during my first semester I attended a Christian conference. The topic was evangelism, and I went along hoping it would alleviate my fears and give me the courage I sorely lacked.

The first talk was on the biblical imperative of evangelism, and I felt both inspired and convicted. In the second talk, though, I began to struggle. The topic was "How to be a witness," and the speaker made three points:

- Share the gospel with as many people as possible in a day. He offered some stock phrases to introduce the topic.
- Always press for a commitment to Christ. If they aren't interested, then move on to another person.
- Regard their questions as smokescreens—things people use to avoid considering faith. Answer their questions if possible, but realize that their questions probably indicate a lack of spiritual openness.

We were sent to a local shopping center with instructions to speak to as many people as possible about Jesus. We weren't to dawdle in conversation but to seek to lead them to Christ.

I decided to follow my own instincts, however, and spent the entire afternoon having a stimulating spiritual conversation with only one person. I didn't press her for a commitment to Christ because it seemed premature. At the end of our conversation we exchanged addresses in order to continue our spiritual dialogue.

Back at the conference we had a large group "sharing time" about how our afternoon had gone. I realized that "success" was being defined by how many people had made professions of faith, and by those standards I had failed. Yet I still felt very positive about the spiritual conversation I had had that afternoon.

These conference speakers were faithful, sincere believers who loved the Lord. Yet I left the conference not only confused but with more questions than when I arrived! What does it mean to be a witness to Jesus? How did Jesus talk to people about faith? Is conversion the only measure of evangelistic "success"? Are "results" even something we can make happen anyway?

I came away from that conference convinced of two things: that, yes, God calls us to be his witnesses, but also that now I had to investigate how Jesus talked to others about faith.

So I began poring over the Gospels. I was deeply struck by Jesus' tremendous compassion for people. He demonstrated respect by listening carefully to others. He asked provocative questions and was unabashedly persuasive in a way that seemed to rouse people's curiosity so that they wanted to hear more.

No matter how pressing were the demands in Jesus' life, he was never in a rush to move on to the next person. He never treated people as evangelistic "projects." Nor did he share the gospel with everyone in exactly the same way. Even the way Jesus spoke about faith—the metaphors and illustrations he used—was dependent upon the person he was speaking to. He didn't even "give the gospel" to every person he met.

I discovered no formulas: no three set questions that Jesus always used with everyone. I gained tremendous insight by watching how Jesus spoke about faith, but it was also clear that he witnessed on a case-by-case basis.

I wanted to learn how to share my faith in the way that Jesus did. So I asked God to guide me to people that he was seeking: in my dorm, in my classes, where my life naturally intersected with people. I always kept my dorm-room door open. I reached out to all types of people: those who seemed quite far from God's kingdom and those who were very different from me.

Every day I asked God to fill me afresh with his love and compassion for others. I invited unbelievers to do things with me socially. I asked them questions to better understand who they were and what their obstacles to faith were. I began to casually drop mention of God into ordinary conversation to see if it might spark their curiosity in faith, the way I had seen Jesus do. I prayed that God would use me. Most of all, I asked God to open their eyes and draw them to the beauty and wonder of the gospel.

It did not take long to develop genuine friendships with skeptics who shared their lives with me, as I did mine with them. As we engaged in conversation, I learned their views on various issues, which enabled me to understand better their underlying core beliefs. Eventually they began asking me what I believed. I told them why Jesus was so irresistibly attractive to me and how I had come to believe that Christianity was true.

As I was preparing to go home for Christmas break, three students on my dorm floor came to me and said, "Becky, the way you talk about faith makes us very curious. None of us have read the Bible before. Would you be willing to explore the Bible with us? We want to understand what you saw that changed your life so much."

I turned them down flat.

To my shame now, I told them I was very new to faith and was in no way competent to lead a Bible study. "I know so little about the Bible myself!" I said. To which they responded, "Then we'll learn together!" They asked me three times before I finally agreed, reluctantly.

All during Christmas break I worried, panicked, and prayed. The only conclusion I could reach was that God had instigated this. On our first week back the four of us met to read a Bible story about Jesus.

To say I was an inept Bible-study leader would be a vast under-statement. I had never even been in a Bible study, much less led one! Simply choosing the passages was a challenge for me. To my amazement, they enjoyed it—and so did I. By the second week one more student had joined us, and by the third week we were six.

If you had asked me then what my view was of evangelism, I would have said, "I am amazed to say this, but evangelism isn't that hard! If you pray, if you are authentic and truly care about people… and if you listen respectfully and try to understand their questions and difficulties with faith and you're willing to share your beliefs… you'll find that having spiritual conversations is something you both enjoy! The truth is, evangelism is much easier than I thought!"

I still believe this. Even today, as our Western culture grows increasingly hostile to faith and the challenges in evangelism are significant, I truly think sharing our faith is easier than we tend to assume. Skeptics often respond to genuine love and appreciate our desire for respectful dialogue. The truth is, people are hungry for something they can't quite name—but it is there.

Then I had a second experience. Things were about to get harder.

EXPERIENCING THE HOSTILITY

On the evening of our third Bible study I returned to my dorm room and heard, along with everyone else, an announcement over the public P.A. system asking me to come immediately to the dorm advisor's office. The dorm advisor was a middle-aged woman who lived in an apartment on the ground floor. As I entered her room and saw the look on her face, I knew that whatever it was, it was serious.

"Becky, is it true you are leading a Bible study in the dorm?" she asked.

"Yes."

"Well, it's against our dorm policy to do this, and one student has already registered a complaint," she said.

I was flabbergasted. "But I wasn't coercing people to come. In fact, they asked me to lead it!"

"Becky, I've already had meetings about this with my colleagues from other dorms. I am telling you: shut it down NOW!"

"But why? Is it breaking dorm policy to lead a Bible study that the students themselves asked for?" I wasn't being cocky. I was terrified, but genuinely puzzled.

"Listen, Becky," she said. "You're young. I don't know how you got mixed up with this religious thing. I really like you, but you could be in serious trouble. In fact, if you persist in doing this, you might be asked to leave this university. So for your own sake, stop it now!"

"I could be kicked out of the university?" I asked incredulously.

"That is exactly what I'm saying," she answered.

Two things raced through my mind. First, my dad was not a Christian. In fact, at that time, apart from my sister, I was the only committed Christian in my family. The shame I would feel at being sent home from university in this way was too excruciating to face.

Second, I realized that I hadn't prayed. So I silently cried out to the Lord for help. I will never forget the peace that instantly flooded me. Then I spoke words that I knew were given to me by God.

"I want to honor this university and obey its rules. I truly want to be respectful. But I cannot stop this Bible study. I must do what I feel God has led me to do. How can I not speak about what I know to be true?"

"I am very sorry to hear this, Becky," the dorm advisor replied. "I will now have to take this to a higher level. I will be in touch with you soon. But you are being very foolish. Will you agree not to invite any more students to come until we have our next meeting?"

"Remember, I didn't invite anyone in the first place. But, yes, I agree," I said.

I went back to my dorm room, threw myself on the bed and began sobbing. I remember saying to the Lord, "Lord, you are invisible! People can't see you, but they can see me. And if I'm expelled from university, then *you* will have to explain this to my dad!"

A student friend, Paula, came to my room wanting to know why I'd been summoned by the dorm advisor. I told her and, seeing my distress, she said, "Becky, my dad is an elder at our church. Come home with me this weekend and talk it over with him."

That weekend her father listened to my story with great compassion and said, "Becky, I don't believe they can expel you. But you've been hit hard, and it was a very frightening experience. This afternoon I want you to read the book of Acts, all the way through. It will help you. Then we'll talk about it."

Stifling my sobs, I dutifully wrote down the title and asked him where I could buy the book.

"Um… Becky, the book of Acts is in the Bible, right after the Gospels," he said. Then with a wry smile he added, "This must be quite some Bible study you are leading!"

That afternoon, for the first time in my life, I read Acts. I will never forget reading Acts 4 v 18-21, when Peter and John were hauled before the Jewish authorities and threatened for preaching the gospel:

> Then they called them in again and commanded them not to speak or teach at all in the name of Jesus. But Peter and John replied, "Which is right in God's eyes: to listen to you, or to him? You be the judges! As for us, we cannot help speaking about what we have seen and heard." After further threats they let them go.

As I read Peter and John's response, my eyes grew as large as saucers. I rose from my chair and said out loud, "Lord, that is almost exactly what I just said to my dorm advisor!"

My first reaction in reading Acts was shock at discovering that my experience wasn't new. Christians have always been persecuted. My second reaction was deep shame. The apostles were not only harassed for sharing the gospel—all but one of them would die as martyrs for doing so. They experienced a level of persecution I never had and likely never would. I confessed my fears to God and asked him to strengthen me to be obedient and faithful, no matter what the outcome.

I returned to campus feeling renewed and strengthened. On Tuesday evening as I walked to the students' room where we met for the Bible study, I was surprised to see the hall filled with students.

"Excuse me," I said. "I need to get through because I have a meeting."

"That's where we're going too," they said. "Only, the room isn't big enough. We can't all fit in!"

They were all trying to go to my Bible study!

I was horrified. Despite Paula's dad's reassurances, I wasn't at all convinced that I wouldn't be expelled from the university. While I was determined to be obedient, I was still hoping that since the Bible study was small, there would be no more trouble. But there were over ten women in the hall alone!

What had happened?! Well, this was the late sixties, the height of the "revolutionary protest" among young people in the US. "Don't trust anyone over 30" was a popular mantra. And so my story had travelled like wildfire. News that the administration was trying to shut down anything—even a Bible study—fed into the revolution- ary spirit of the age. The following week even more women came! We finally had to meet in the only available public room on our floor that was large enough to accommodate us. Their interest in coming was probably far more motivated by their desire to stick it to the university than to wrestle with the claims of Christianity. Nevertheless, they came and heard about Jesus.

Of course, I was summoned by the dorm advisor, who was furious.

"Becky, I told you not to invite anyone else until we had our next meeting!"

"But I didn't invite anyone! Students began inviting other students!"

She didn't look convinced, and she issued more threats, saying that my expulsion from the university was now almost inevitable.

The comic irony is that I was hoping to keep a lid on things by keeping the study small. But the more she threatened me, the more she fanned the flame of the students' protest. This Bible study, taking place in the "Bible Belt," had ended up being seen as counter-cultural and revolutionary! But, in a real sense, that is precisely what any study of Scripture is—in any place and any age.

A few days later, as I was walking through the coffee shop in the Student Union, a student in the Bible study called me over and introduced me to an older man sitting at the table. He said he had just been told about the Bible-study situation and asked me to explain what had happened. After listening to my story he said, "Becky, I am the minister at a Unitarian church here in town. Would you be willing to come this Sunday and simply tell your story in place of my sermon?"

I tried to decline, but he was insistent, so in the end I decided to agree. But I was concerned—Unitarians deny the existence of the Trinity, one of the truths at the very heart of true Christian belief. I went to a mature Christian student friend, Lydia, and asked her if I'd made a mistake accepting.

"Becky," said Lydia. "I believe the Lord has provided a real opportunity for you to proclaim the gospel. But don't just share what happened. Be sure to share your testimony as well."

"I will," I answered. "But, um… what's a testimony?"

"It's how you came to Christ. Tell your story of being an agnostic and how you had lots of intellectual questions—how you looked at other religions before exploring Christianity. Share why the gospel ultimately made so much sense to you."

Sunday morning came and I was beyond terrified. But as I began speaking, I felt the same peace that I had experienced when the dorm advisor had confronted me. After the service I discovered that many members of the church were from the university faculty. Four professors came up to me and gave me their cards and said, "We will help you in any way we can. Call us if you have any more trouble."

The dorm advisor and I had one last meeting, but this time I knew her threats were empty. I will never know what motivated her actions.

EASIER AND HARDER

What did I learn from my first year at university, all those years ago? First, that when evangelism is done the "Jesus way," it is far easier than I could have imagined. Some of the most unlikely people turned out to be the most spiritually hungry.

Second, I learned that sharing the gospel is deadly serious. I had worried that I might offend a skeptic or be accused of being anti-intellectual. Never did I imagine that I would be brought before the dorm advisor, forbidden to invite anyone else to the Bible study, and threatened with expulsion from the university.

What was really going on, even back then in the late 1960s and in the heart of the Bible Belt? I was experiencing something I had never heard of: spiritual warfare. It felt as if I'd been caught in the crossfire of a battle that wasn't of my own making. I had read about Satan in the Bible, but now I knew firsthand that there is indeed a malevolent being who is fiercely opposed to Christ being proclaimed and who will threaten, intimidate, harass, and use every scare tactic possible to get us to stop. And with me, it had nearly worked.

I learned another invaluable lesson: not only is God delighted when we make the gospel known—he will multiply our

"Not only is God delighted when we make the gospel known—he will multiply our efforts."

efforts—even when we don't really want him to! Being threatened with expulsion was terrifying. Even though I chose to obey, I was still hoping that I could "manage" the danger by keeping the Bible study small. Instead, God opened the floodgates! Every tactic that Satan used to suppress the gospel God used to make the gospel more widely known.

The lessons I learned through that experience have sustained and shaped me throughout my entire ministry. While many things have changed between the sixties and today, the one thing that remains the same is this:

> *Evangelism is still easier than we think and harder than we imagine: it is both exciting and deadly serious.*

In today's cultural climate we will need courage, endurance, and practical equipping to be effective witnesses. But we also need confidence and a sense of expectation. As the British evangelist Rico Tice puts it:

> "There is increasing hostility to the gospel message [today]. But something else is going on, too. There is also increased hunger. The same rising tide of secularism and materialism that rejects truth claims and is offended by absolute moral standards is proving to be an empty and hollow way to live. And that means that, excitingly, you're more and more likely to find people quietly hungering for the content of the gospel."
>
> (*Honest Evangelism*, page 20)

Most of all we need to start with God, because all of our struggles in evangelism—our deep sense of inadequacy and weakness, our fears, our feelings of spiritual poverty in prayer, our secret doubts as to whether the gospel has the power to transform lives, our uncertainty that God could really use us, and our deep-down unwillingness to take the risks and put ourselves in the situations where God might use us—can only be overcome by first understanding who God truly is. Knowing that God is with us, that he goes before us, and that he intends to use us, even with our fears and our sometimes-flagging faith, is what makes all the difference. As the 19th-century preacher Charles Spurgeon said, "Some are babes, and others are giants. But ... little faith is blessed faith. Trembling hope is blessed hope" (*Faith's Checkbook*, crosswalk. com/devotionals/faithcheckbook, Feb 21st devotional, accessed 12/23/19).

The truth is, it is not self-confidence we need. What we need, more than anything else, is God-confidence. Having confidence in the true God is what enables us to see that our weakness does not limit the powerful living God. He is delighted to use us, as we take small steps of obedience.

Jesus commands us to be his witnesses. It's going to be easier than we think and harder than we imagine. But Jesus does not send us out empty-handed. He gives us the divine means we need to obey his divine command—and those means are what the first section of this book is all about.

QUESTIONS FOR REFLECTION

- Think back to your own experiences of trying to share the gospel with others. How have they shaped your expectations of and feelings about evangelism?

- What did you learn from Becky about how Jesus approached people with the gospel? How could you implement Jesus' approach in your own witness?
- "It is not self-confidence we need. What we need, more than anything else, is God-confidence." Do you tend to move forwards relying on yourself or to doubt yourself and not move forwards? How does that trait influence your attitude toward sharing your faith?

CHAPTER TWO

CELEBRATING OUR SMALLNESS

When I was an agnostic, there was one question I continually wrestled with: "How can finite limited human beings ever claim they know God? How do they know they are not being deceived?"

One sunny summer day I was stretched out on the lawn in the back garden of my home when I noticed that some ants were busy building a mound. I began to redirect their steps with twigs and leaves. But they simply bounced off and started a new ant mound. I thought, "This is like being God! I am redirecting their steps, and they don't even realize it!"

At one point, two ants crawled onto my hand and I thought, "Wouldn't it be funny if one ant turned to the other ant and said, 'Do you believe in Becky? Do you believe Becky really exists?'"

I imagined the other ant answering, "Don't be ridiculous! Becky is a myth, a fairy tale!" "How comical," I thought—the hubris of that ant declaring that I don't exist, when I could easily blow it off my hand!

But what if the other ant said, "Oh, I believe that Becky exists!" How would they resolve it? "How could they know that I am real?" I thought. "What would I have to do to reveal to them who I am?"

Suddenly I realized: the only way to reveal who I am, in a way that they could understand, would be to become an ant myself. I would have to identify totally with their sphere of reality.

I sat upright, and I remember thinking, "What an amazing thought! The scaling-down of the size of me to perfectly represent who I am in the form of an ant! But how would the ants know they were actually seeing me in the form of an ant? I know; I would have to do tricks! Things that no other ant could do!"

Then it hit me: I had just solved my problem of how finite creatures could ever discover God. God would have to come from the outside and reveal who he is.

At that point, I had not looked into Christianity. But I had looked at other world religions, and I knew that I had not read of a founder or prophet saying to their followers, "Don't you understand? When you look at me you are looking at God, because I am God!" Instead, they turned their followers' attention away from themselves and spoke of the importance of following rules and engaging in certain spiritual practices in order to, perhaps, achieve acceptance or salvation from God.

Now I needed to know if the Bible claimed that God came to earth in human form. I couldn't find a Bible in our home, so I searched for any book that had the word "Christian" in its title, and I found one! It was an unread copy of *Mere Christianity*, so I sat down and began reading voraciously.

What did I discover? The very premise of the Christian faith is that God performed a supernatural break-in on Planet Earth! Christianity is a religion of revelation. God came to us! Just as I had imagined becoming an ant while still remaining Becky so that I could communicate to the ants, so Christ had assumed human nature while still remaining his divine self so that he could communicate with us!

I was not convinced yet that Christianity was true, but this approach made sense to me. If God did exist, then surely he would reveal himself in a way that we could understand.

C.S. Lewis also sparked my curiosity in reading the Bible. I started with the Gospels, and I will never forget reading for the first time…

> The Word became flesh and made his dwelling among us. We have seen his glory, the glory of the one and only Son, who came from the Father, full of grace and truth … Grace and truth came through Jesus Christ. No one has ever seen God, but the one and only Son, who is himself God and is in closest relationship with the Father, has made him known. (John 1 v 14, 17-18)

It was a process, but I eventually came to believe that Jesus was who he said: the Son of God sent to our planet because we were in desperate trouble. Jesus came and not only revealed the Father to us; he took on our sin by dying on the cross. One day I gave my life to God through Jesus Christ, fully and unreservedly.

ON BEING HUMAN

Knowing God was one part of my search, but discovering who we are and why we are here was the other. I was surprised to discover that not only is Jesus our window into understanding God's nature, but he also reveals what it means to be truly human: human in the way God intended.

In all my years of ministry I have wrestled deeply with why Christians struggle to share their faith. I always knew it was not because they lacked the latest, greatest technique or some new formula that worked on one and all (there were and still are plenty of people around offering those kinds of evangelistic "strategies"). Over time I began to see that the problem was deeper.

Dick and I have travelled the world equipping Christians in the area of evangelism, and what is the one thing we most consistently hear? People come up to us during a conference, looking as if they are about to confess their darkest secret: something they hope no one will ever discover. And they say, "I really want to share my faith—but I just can't."

"Why can't you?" we always ask.

"Because," they say, looking around hoping no one is listening, "I just don't know enough. I am not a perfect example of a Christian. And what if I offend them? What if I can't answer their questions? The bottom line is, I can't share my faith because… I'm so inadequate!"

"Well, of course you're inadequate!" we answer: "We're all inadequate! All of us are completely dependent upon God! And isn't it freeing to know? There is no shame in depending on God!"

What their comments reveal is a failure to understand how God created us. To put it another way, we do not understand what it means to be human. We forget that, as the old children's hymn says, "They (we) are weak but he is strong."

This is such a simple idea, and yet it is precisely where we stumble. Throughout history, humans have struggled to accept the fact that we are creatures, not the Creator—that we are weak, yes, but that he is strong. Yet understanding this distinction makes all the difference in how we live our lives; it relieves our anxiety, brings us peace, and it will help us enormously in our witness for Christ.

Where do we go to discover what it means to be human in the way God intended? We need to start where the Bible starts: with the story of creation.

Genesis 1 and 2 tell the wonderful story of the beginning of all things. The sovereign God created the universe: "God said, 'Let there be' ... and there was ... and God saw that it was good" (Genesis 1 v 3, 9). Only when he created human beings did God deliberate about what and how to create. For the first time in the story God uses a blueprint. The blueprint is God's own self: "Let us make mankind in our image, in our likeness" (Genesis 1 v 26). God made humans to reflect God's nature so that we can know, serve, and glorify him, but with this critical distinction: we are creatures, not the Creator! The fact that God created us means the foundation of human existence is not in ourselves, because the purpose and meaning of our lives is not determined by us but given to us by God. The author and apologist Ravi Zacharias sums up what it means to be human like this: that "we are created in the image of God for the glorious reality of being in permanent fellowship with him." To be a human creature, created to depend upon and discover our meaning from and with God, is "very good"—God says so (Genesis 1 v 31)! Yet it is one of the first things that Satan seeks to dismantle.

DENYING WE'RE HUMAN

In Genesis 3 we learn that evil was already present on earth. The Bible doesn't tell us much about how this came about, but the source of evil is identified throughout the Bible as Satan (meaning "adversary"). The Bible describes Satan as a created spiritual being: a fallen angel who rebelled against God in heaven and was cast out. He became a malevolent spiritual being, the father of lies and a master of disguise whose desire is to blind people to God's truth (John 8 v 44; 2 Corinthians 4 v 4).

When Satan approached Adam and Eve to tempt them in the garden, his presence was disguised and hidden in the snake. The snake said, "Did God really say, 'You must not eat from any tree in the garden?'" (Genesis 3 v 1). This simple-sounding question masks an evil brilliance. The sixteenth-century Reformer Martin Luther said that he found that verse almost impossible to translate from the original language into German because it is so devilishly clever.

By beginning in such a seemingly innocent way, the devil plants the suggestion that surely God would not say this—not the God who loves these humans? Yet look behind the question and we see a masked implication lurking: that God created us in order to starve us to death! Which can only mean that God must be a sadist! Yet God never said, "You must not eat from any tree in the garden." God had told them they could eat freely of all the trees except for one (2 v 16-17). Through this tiny insinuation the snake is saying that God does not have their best interests at heart—that God is actually holding out on them! Satan wants them to doubt God's goodness and love so that their faith in God will be poisoned.

Eve corrects the snake by saying that God only forbade them to eat from the one tree: "But God did say, 'You must not eat fruit from [that] tree … and you must not touch it, or you will die" (3 v 3). Now the snake knows that his strategy is working! Why? Because God never said they cannot touch the fruit. By overstating God's strictness Eve reveals that she is falling for the lie that God isn't good and is actually depriving them. Thus Eve becomes the first legalist in history.

Now the snake engages in outright contradiction: "You will not die ... for God knows that when you eat of it your eyes will be opened, and you will be like God..." (3 v 4-5). *Eve, don't you get it?* the snake is saying. *God is envious and he clearly can't stand any competition. He couldn't bear it if you were to become God too!*

Everything is turned upside down. Divine love is presented as jealousy and fulfillment in service to God as servility. Because Satan resents God being in charge and having all the power, his chief argument, which lies behind everything he says, is this: *Being God is everything—it is all that matters; being creatures who are dependent upon God is a state to be avoided, fought against, and escaped from. Therefore, reject your humanity and be God!*

Satan is doing two things at once: he is attacking God's character, and he is denying the goodness of who God created us to be: creatures. It's a horrific demonic lie that stands in direct contrast to everything we have learned in Genesis 1 and 2: that God is good and trustworthy and that being a human being, created to depend upon a loving and good God, is precious and wonderful!

Satan wants us, instead of celebrating our human dependence upon God, to hate the fact that God is God and we are not. He wants us to despise our "smallness" and to view it as an embarrassment. But recognizing our inadequacy and dependence upon God isn't shameful—it is what sets us free! Being creatures isn't "rubbish," as Satan wants us to believe. Being creatures who love, obey, and depend upon God without shame is glorious.

In Genesis 3, evil gains ground through the refusal of human creatures to be who they truly are: beings created by God out of his immense love and joy, and who find fulfillment and freedom through their dependence upon their loving and merciful God.

THE PROBLEM PERSISTS

Take a long look at the depths of human insecurity since human beings first believed Satan's lie in Genesis 3 and you will see that that lie has taken deep root. We use cures and self-help formulas to try to overcome our sense of inadequacy. The late psychiatrist Wilhelm Reich, having done psychotherapy with people for decades, concluded: "What is the dynamic of human misery on this planet? It all stems from man trying to be other than he is" (*The Mass Psychology of Fascism*, page 234).

This is a brilliant secular explanation of how sin manifests itself! Reich, however, does not answer why we try to appear more than we are, because that is something that only God our Creator can reveal. The biblical answer is that we are rebels who, in our heart of hearts, know we are not God but wish we were! So we hide our inadequacy by trying to appear to be more than we really are. The prophet Ezekiel says it best: "Though you are a man and no god, you try to think the thoughts of a god" (Ezekiel 28 v 2, NEB).

Past history and current culture are littered with examples that prove Ezekiel's point. Consider Yuval Noah Harari's bestseller *Sapiens*, in which Harari writes that, due to genetic engineering humans are on the verge of overcoming natural selection and becoming gods. Yet, he ironically notes, we still seem unhappy and in many ways unsure of what we want: "Is there anything more dangerous than dissatisfied and irresponsible gods [us] who don't know what they want?" (page 443).

As Christians, we know that we are not God. Yet we easily fall into the trap of feeling embarrassed about being God-dependent people. We do not want our weakness or the limits of our humanity ever to be exposed. So we try to never appear foolish or say anything that could be construed as anti-intellectual or out of step with our culture. We fear human judgment more than God's. Isn't this why we are often so reluctant to share our faith? Because, we fear, it may expose our weakness or may make us look foolish?

We need to accept the limitations of our humanity. And we can do so by looking at the birth of Jesus.

POWER IN WEAKNESS

As the shepherds were watching their flocks by night, Luke tells us in his Gospel:

> An angel of the Lord appeared to them, and the glory of the Lord shone around them, and they were terrified. But the angel said to them, "Do not be afraid. I bring you good news that will cause great joy for all the people. Today in the town of David a Savior has been born to you; he is the Messiah, the Lord. This will be a sign to you: You will find a baby wrapped in cloths and lying in a manger."
>
> Suddenly a great company of the heavenly host appeared with the angel, praising God and saying,
>
> "Glory to God in the highest heaven,
>   and on earth peace to those on whom his favor rests."
>
> (Luke 2 v 9-14)

Why were the heavenly host worshiping with such unbridled joy after the angel announced Christ's birth to these astonished, terrified shepherds? Because they knew the identity of the One whom God had sent! As Paul described it, "God was pleased to have all his fullness dwell in him" (Colossians 1 v 19-20).

The heavenly host knew that the coming of the Son of God was unprecedented and would change forever the entire course of human history! Furthermore, they knew that God the Father had for centuries been revealing his plan for the entry of his Son to earth. Which leads us to raise the obvious question: why did God send his Son, who had been accustomed to all the majesty of heaven, into the world in the weakest, humblest way imaginable—as a helpless, utterly dependent baby who was even laid in an animal trough?

First, because God is turning the demonic lie on its head! To be human—to be dependent—is wonderful in God's eyes! That is why we must never despise our smallness, since the Son of God became "small" when he became human. His birth is a tremendous validation of how good it is to be human. Christ becoming flesh "hallows all flesh," as the poet Charles Williams said. Second, the humble circumstances of his birth are a sign that Jesus didn't come to save only the privileged and the powerful; he came to save all of humanity.

The fact that Christ came in the utter weakness and vulnerability of a baby has immense significance when it comes to evangelism. Here's why: Jesus' birth reveals that God is pleased to dwell in and reveal his glory through human weakness. That is a theme throughout all of Scripture. All through the Bible we see that there is a profound relationship between human weakness and God's power.

Consider the apostle Paul, one the greatest evangelists in history. How did Paul feel as he went on his missionary journey to the important city of Corinth, the "Sin City" of the ancient world? Was he brimming with self-confidence? In 1 Corinthians 2 v 3-5 we read Paul's own view—and it gives us an invaluable insight into why recognizing our smallness is actually a gift:

I came to you in weakness with great fear and trembling. My message and my preaching were not with wise and persuasive words, but with a demonstration of the Spirit's power, so that your faith might not rest on human wisdom, but on God's power.

Paul's statement is staggering. Paul says he glories in his weakness and inadequacy so that Christ's power may be revealed. This is the very antithesis of Genesis 3! Satan wants us to detest the fact that being human means we must depend upon God. But Paul says the exact opposite! He says that he has learned to love and celebrate his weakness because through his inadequacy God's power and grace are revealed.

But how do we learn to live like this? Paul shows us that the answer lies in first accepting our smallness. This is about much more than acknowledging our limitations. It means experiencing a power much greater than our own and surrendering to it, which we will look at in a later chapter. Learning to accept our humanness is what leads us to depend upon God's strength. It puts us in a position where we are able to joyfully accept that God has all the strength and power we could ever need, and we don't—and so we're going to need his help!

Someone who has taught me and countless others how to view human weakness through God's eyes is the renowned author and speaker Joni Eareckson Tada. Joni had a diving accident when she was a teenager that resulted in her becoming disabled with quadriplegia. God has used Joni to be his witness in extraordinary ways ever since. I have known Joni for a long time, so when she came to speak at our church, I asked her if we could have lunch together, and said I would bring a packed lunch.

As we sat alone together in one of the rooms, it suddenly occurred to me that I would need to help her. So I picked up the sandwich and began to feed her. I put the straw to her mouth so she could drink. I wiped her mouth with the napkin. It's hard to describe the intimacy of that lunch. The only time I had ever fed anyone was when my children were babies or when I visited my grandmother in her nursing home. In other words, I had only done this for those who were at the opposite ends of the human lifespan.

This time, though, I wasn't feeding my babies or my grandmother—I was feeding the remarkable, heroic Joni Tada. The act of feeding her felt almost sacred. Somehow her physical weakness caused me to feel at ease with my own human weakness. Before long I began telling her about the challenges I was facing and where I was waiting on the Lord for answers. And she did the same.

I reflected on that experience for a long time afterwards. Why did feeding Joni lunch have such a profound effect on me? Eventually I concluded that it was because I was in the presence of a woman who had made peace with her weakness. The blessing of her physical disability, I have heard her say, is the constant reminder that we are God-dependent and not self-sufficient people. What she said in her lecture that day was enlightening:

> "I'm no expert at being disabled. It's hard. It's inconvenient. Every morning when my helpers come to get me up, I take a deep breath and pray, 'Ok Lord, show up for me big time. I need you, Jesus, very much today.' It's a daily, hard-fought-for, desperate pulling down of grace from heaven. But we must learn to turn to God in all circumstances and say, 'I can do things only

through your strengthening power. So help me Lord
and strengthen me—not just for witnessing opportunities, but for every minute and every second.'"

When we learn to celebrate our smallness and to depend upon
the power of God, it affects every aspect of our lives. And that
includes our sharing of the gospel—because it diminishes our
fears when we realize that it is ok to be inadequate, that being
able to answer every question skeptics ask is not required,
and, most of all, that our human weakness is no hindrance
to God using us for his kingdom to spread the glorious good
news. As Paul said (and it's what I need to recall every time I
share my faith), "[God's] power is made perfect in weakness"
(2 Corinthians 12 v 9). Therefore, "accepting your inadequacy
is the first qualification to being used by God!" (John Gaynor
Banks, *The Master and the Disciple*, quoted in Leanne Payne, *The
Healing Presence*, page 21).

So, the next time you consider witnessing to a neighbor or
a family member or a work colleague, and you think, "I can't,
because…" don't let that defeat you. But equally, don't try to find
the confidence or ability within you. Yes, you're inadequate. And
when you accept that you're a dependent creature, with a mighty
Creator, then you're in the place where he can use you. We are
weak, yet he is strong.

QUESTIONS FOR REFLECTION

- In what ways can you acknowledge and celebrate your
  dependence on God? In what ways do you find yourself
  fighting the idea that you are dependent?

- "God's power is made perfect in weakness." How have you experienced the truth of this in your own life?
- How does knowing that God uses us in our weakness strengthen you in evangelism? If you instinctively resist that idea, why is that, do you think?

CHAPTER THREE

GLORY IN THE WEAKNESS

Here lies the greatest surprise in all of history: ever since the entry of sin into this world, humanity has been on a mad course to try to become God… while God had decided from the beginning of time to become human!

In his extravagant love, the triune God chose to unite himself to his creation in the closest of all possible unions—by becoming that which he had already created! Imagine it: the Infinite became finite; the Eternal entered time; the Invisible became visible; and the Creator became a created being.

We've seen that we are created to be creatures, not the Creator. We've seen that the Father sent the Son not as a triumphant King in full regalia but as a baby who was placed in an animal feeding trough. All of which points us to the importance of accepting our "smallness" as human beings. Yet we've also seen that there is another aspect to being human, which Paul wrote about to the Corinthian church: that God's power and glory is revealed through our human weakness, which is why we can celebrate our smallness!

But since the fall, this view of ourselves has never come to us naturally. So who can teach us how to accept the limits of our humanness without shame and to celebrate the fact that God's power and glory are manifested through our weakness? Amazingly, the answer is Jesus! But how can the divine Son of God truly understand what it means to be human? Because Jesus came to us as fully divine and yet fully human, though without sin. Of course, Jesus' nature is a mystery which cannot be fully comprehended by our human minds. Nevertheless, it is worth probing, because once we grasp that God's glory works through our weakness, it will make a huge difference to our fears about evangelism, especially our fear of inadequacy.

HOW TO BE HUMAN

In the 1980s fantasy film *Cocoon,* the American actor Brian Dennehy plays an extraterrestrial on a mission to retrieve other ETs who, on a prior visit, have been left behind in pods on the sea floor. His purpose is simply to retrieve them and take them back on his space ship. So he and his team move the pods to a private swimming pool, in a neighborhood near a senior citizen center.

Their main challenge, of course, is how to disguise themselves so they can accomplish their mission. Dennehy's character looks like a human being. But one day, when he mistakenly thinks no one is around, he unzips his brilliantly crafted human suit. As it falls off, some elderly people who are hidden from his view completely freak out when they see that he is actually a being of pure light. His human appearance isn't real. He is another creature altogether.

It is easy, but mistaken, to assume that this is what Jesus was like: a divine being covered with human skin. Yes, we know that Jesus walked to different cities in Galilee, but he could have flown if he wanted to, right? Yes, he ate meals with people, but that was just to be friendly because he didn't need to eat food to live, did he? Yes, he prayed, but that was kind of just a good example—he already knew the answer anyway, surely.

Throughout church history we have tended either to over-emphasize Christ's deity and diminish his humanity or (as in today's culture) the reverse. But Jesus wasn't masquerading as a human being. He wasn't 90% divine and 10% human, nor did he exchange his divinity for his humanity. Jesus was fully God and fully human. He had two natures—divine and human—in one person.

At the start of John's Gospel, the apostle testifies to Christ's divine nature: "In the beginning was the Word [Christ], and the Word was with God and the Word was God. He was with God in the beginning" (John 1 v 1-2). John also tells us that "Through him all things were made; without him nothing was made that has been made." That means that Christ, the divine Son of God, created the galaxies and formed the cosmos, the moon, the sun and the stars. Before he came to our planet, he lived outside our sensory experience and was a transcendent being.

As we've seen, John also testified to Christ's humanity: "The Word became flesh and made his dwelling among us. We have seen his glory" (John 1 v 14). Paul says that Christ was "in very nature God, [yet he] did not consider equality with God something to be grasped, but made himself nothing, taking the very nature of a servant, being made in human likeness" (Philippians 2 v 6-7, NIV1984). The Son was fully human, sharing our human limitations of time, space, knowledge, and mortality—though not our sin, for that was not part of God's design for us when he made humanity.

In other words, when Jesus came to earth he not only revealed God's divine character; he also showed us what it means to be fully human. For example, in the Gospels Jesus shows us the following human characteristics.

The fullness of true human affections: Jesus loved people. Even on the cross, when he was experiencing immense suffering, Jesus loved his mother by asking his disciple John to care for her as his own mother.

The fullness of true human emotions: The Gospel stories reveal that Jesus wept and was grieved. He could be amazed and he was moved to compassion. And Jesus suffered, as we see so vividly in his experience in the Garden of Gethsemane and in his death on the cross.

The fullness of true human choice: He became human by choice; he chose not to surrender to temptation; he chose to go to the cross.

The fullness of true human development and intellect: It is an amazing thought to consider that his mother, Mary, would have taught Jesus his colors as a child: "Jesus, this is blue. This is red." Joseph would have taught him the necessary skills to be a carpenter. Jesus grew in stature and wisdom because that is what humans are created to do (Luke 2 v 52).

The fullness of true human bodily experience: Jesus became tired, and thirsty, and hungry, as we see in the story of the Samaritan woman in John 4.

The fullness of true human dependence upon God: When Jesus was born on earth, he did not lay aside his deity, but he did lay aside his glory and majesty. In other words, Jesus did not exercise all of his divine capabilities. For example:

- When Jesus was arrested in the garden by armed guards, he said, "Do you think I cannot call on my Father and he will at once put at my disposal more than twelve legions of angels? But how then would the Scriptures be fulfilled that say it must happen in this way?" (Matthew 26 v 53). He could have depended on angelic armies, but he was also a human who depended, as all humans must, upon God.

- When Jesus was about to choose his disciples, he did not say, *Father, tomorrow is a very big day. Could you give me twelve names quickly so I can get some rest?* Instead Jesus did what we must do. He wrestled through the night in prayer in order to know the Father's will before selecting them: "One of those nights Jesus went out to a mountainside to pray, and spent the night praying to God. When morning came he called his disciples to him" (Luke 6 v 12-13).

- When Satan tempted Jesus in the wilderness, Jesus did not say, *Excuse me, but you can't do this because I am God's Son.* Instead Jesus willingly experienced temptation, identifying with our human experience not theoretically but fully and completely; and he overcame temptation by using the same resources that God has given to all believers: the word of God and the Holy Spirit (Luke 4 v 1-13).

In other words, Jesus didn't press a "God button" to get instant help, which he could have done as God's Son. Instead, by assuming our human nature, he willingly accepted our human limitations. In doing this, he showed us how to live a life of faith and obedience to God.

It is almost impossible to appreciate the depth to which Jesus humbled himself by assuming our human nature. What Jesus shows us so very vividly is that we are created to be God-dependent, not self-sufficient. That is why Jesus was never ashamed by his

"Our weakness and inadequacy are no hindrance to God working through us."

dependence upon God. He wasn't embarrassed that he needed to pray for guidance, or ashamed that he became tired or hungry—because that is what it means to be human.

JUST AS WE ARE

So if Jesus accepted his dependence upon God without embarrassment, then clearly we must accept our dependence as well. Of course, we may think we already do this. But do we really? I would argue that in all of God's creation it is only human beings who struggle to accept their true form. And the more successful we are in life, the harder that is!

Think about it: have you ever noticed that dogs don't get mad about not being cats? Squirrels aren't envious just because they are not cows. The moon is not resentful that it isn't the sun. The truth is that in all God's creation it is only human beings who resent their form. Why? Because our dependent nature always reminds us that we are not God! We want to walk into situations—including proclaiming the gospel—as all-knowing, all-powerful beings, totally in charge and in control at all times. We are secretly frustrated, or at least embarrassed, because our inadequacy means that we must always depend upon God.

Yet what Jesus so beautifully demonstrates is that our joy comes from realizing that we are inadequate and not resenting that; and that God is completely adequate and accepting that with joy! The wonderful news is that our weakness and inadequacy are no hindrance to God working through us. Jesus said, "Blessed are the poor in spirit" (Matthew 5 v 3). In other words, happy are those who see that they are not enough. Why? Because it is only when we see that we are not enough that we are willing to turn to the One who is enough!

So learning to celebrate our smallness is only the first part. We must also learn where true power comes from. God will not help us when we try to live the Christian life in our own strength. It is only when we accept our dependent nature that we see our need to depend upon the power of God—and then God goes to work. We may not know how to reach a person for the gospel—but God does! We will run out of the love we need to love skeptics wisely and well—God does not!

The author John Arnold put it this way in his book *Seeking Peace*:

> "The more confidence we have in our own strength and abilities, the less we are likely to have in Christ. Our human weakness is no hindrance to God. In fact, as long as we do not use it as an excuse for sin, it is good to be weak. But this acceptance of weakness is more than acknowledging our limitations. It is experiencing a power much greater than our own and surrendering to it. As [the twentieth-century German theologian] Eberhard Arnold ... said, 'This is the root of grace—the dismantling of our power ... In my estimation this is the single most important insight with regard to the kingdom of God.'"
>
> (Quoted in Marva J. Dawn, *Powers, Weakness, and the Tabernacling of God*, page 62)

Here is the great truth: God is delighted to use us just as we are—with the questions we can't answer, with our fears and past failures.

We need to keep remembering what the Lord said to Paul: "My grace is sufficient for you, for my power is made perfect through your weakness" (2 Corinthians 12 v 9). We tend to forget (or perhaps we choose not to remember) that God has always used the weak to accomplish his purposes. We think God couldn't use us because we are not smart enough, good enough, or confident enough, and we do not know enough Bible verses—or we think that he will use us only when we are those things. But God has always chosen to use the weak.

Abraham was a moon worshiper from Ur—hardly a great qualification for becoming the father of Israel. David was a shepherd boy who was so undervalued that it didn't even occur to his father to present him to the prophet Samuel—yet he became the greatest king that Israel ever had. The Samaritan women in John 4 had a checkered past and present, yet she became the first Christian convert and (almost immediately) the first evangelist in her community.

Jesus doesn't disqualify us because of our past confessed failures or broken promises. He wants to use us now—where we are, as we are. Why can we go out into the world in weakness, confident of God's strength? Because Jesus, the Lord of lords and the King of kings, came to our planet in weakness. The Lord of the universe, from all his immensity in heaven, became the smallest form of life! Not merely a man, nor a baby nor a fetus. The Lord of the universe, the King of glory, became an embryo!

As the New York pastor and author Tim Keller pointed out in a wonderful sermon I once heard him give, Jesus was willing to come so far down so that we could be brought up—up out of our sin and alienation into a glorious relationship with God. Jesus now offers us his strength and power and wisdom, because, though he came in weakness, he now reigns in heaven.

And he wants to use us to be his witnesses.

STEP ASIDE, BECKY

God has been glorified in my weakness. My faith has grown over the years as I have learned to joyfully confess to God my weakness and my total dependence upon him. I have seen again and again that God knows how to reach my skeptic friends, even when I do not.

When Dick and I were based in the UK so that we could minister throughout Europe, we spent our first three years right outside of Belfast, in a suburb called Holywood. After that we lived for three years in Oxford, and we spent much of our last year in London. At the end of our second year in Holywood, I made a quick appointment for a manicure the day before we were to fly home to Michigan for the summer.

Walking to the salon, I began thinking about the young manicurist whom I had known during those two years. Heather was a lovely, delightful young woman, but not remotely interested in faith. Her interests were primarily in beauty and fashion. She had begun opening up to me about her life, yet whenever I brought up the topic of faith, she always changed the subject. So on my way there that day I prayed, "Lord, I have tried everything to rouse Heather's curiosity in the gospel. But she just isn't interested. If there is a way to reach her, then you, Lord, will have to do it, because I cannot."

Inside the salon there was a shelf against the wall with a tall pile of magazines stacked one on top of the other. Entering, I started to reach for the magazine on top, when I suddenly felt the strong urge to take the magazine in the middle. It was almost as if there was a big arrow pointing to it! Then I went to Heather's table for my manicure.

As she began working on one hand, I started turning pages with my free hand, until I suddenly stopped and stared at one page. I continued turning the pages, but I kept turning back to look at that one page. Heather finally asked, "Why on earth do you keep looking back at that page? What's on it?"

"It's a picture of a very elegant, beautiful woman wearing a gorgeous coat and a hat, but I can't see much of her face," I said. "It's so weird though, because I feel as if I know her... but that's impossible."

Then it suddenly hit me. "Oh my goodness!" I said to Heather: "I do know who she is! It is Jenny Guinness! This picture is a cover from *Vogue* magazine that was taken years ago when she was a well-known fashion model. Later she married my very close friend, Os Guinness."

Heather said, "You know a fashion model who was on the cover of *Vogue*?" As I nodded, she turned to everyone in the salon and said, "Guess what? Becky knows a fashion model whose picture has been on some of the covers of *Vogue*!"

I started to tell Heather of how, during Jenny's career as a fashion model, she began feeling that her life was empty, and how it ultimately led her on a spiritual search. Heather's eyes widened: "Becky, do you know Jenny's story? Because I would love to hear it!"

In that instant I realized what God had done. Fashion and beauty were Heather's "mother ship." To hear anything about the life of a fashion model fascinated her. So I told her about Jenny's search for meaning, what drew her to Christ, and why the gospel had made so much sense to her.

Heather listened in rapt attention. Then she asked me if I had any books on the Christian faith that she could read. Before we left for the airport the next morning, I dropped off some books that were written for seekers.

What does this story tell us? The Lord of the universe, the Maker of heaven and earth, passionately longs for his creation to know him—and that includes a 21-year-old nail technician whose primary interest is fashion. I had walked into the shop saying to the Lord, "I can't reach her, so you must." It was almost as if the Lord was saying, *Step aside, Becky; I will show you how it's done!*

C.S. Lewis, quoting from a poem by Francis Thompson, liked to refer to God as the "Hound of Heaven," because of the way he had pursued Lewis. In his grace and mercy God desires that we collaborate with him in reaching people with the good news of Jesus. His Spirit can nudge us to pick out just the right magazine, because he knows that that magazine will be the very catalyst that will enable us to share the gospel with that particular person. Is there anything more exciting than being in the hands of the living God?!

When we returned to Belfast in the autumn, I discovered that Heather had unexpectedly moved to another country. God had known what I had not—that that appointment had been the last time I would see her. I had asked God to provide an opportunity to share the gospel, and he did! So I entrusted Heather to God's loving care, asking him to bring another Christian into her life who, in God's wonderful timing and grace, may one day lead her to Christ.

Here is the truth we must learn by heart: God uses the weak to reveal his glory! Yes, we are inadequate, but we are also in partnership with the living God! And that changes everything, because he is a God who is delighted to work through the limits of our humanity. What is required from us is not adequacy or self-sufficiency but rather faith in, and obedience and prayer to the God who longs to help us and who will always come to our aid when we ask.

Recognizing and accepting our smallness without shame is the first part. Remembering that God is glorified through our weakness is the next. But we can truly live celebrating our smallness and inadequacy when we understand that it is the Holy Spirit who transcends our limitations—as we will explore in the last chapter in this section.

QUESTIONS FOR REFLECTION

- Which aspects of Jesus' humanity on pages 56-57 most struck you? Which most encouraged you?
- How could you build a conscious reliance on God to help you to love people and share the gospel? How will you pray about these things?
- "God has always chosen to use the weak." How does this truth both encourage and challenge you?

CHAPTER FOUR

WALKING WITH THE SPIRIT

Our planet was changed forever by the birth, death, and resurrection of Jesus Christ. Sometimes we forget there was another glorious event that also changed the earth. It happened seven weeks after the risen Jesus ascended into heaven, during the Jewish festival called Pentecost, when the Lord Jesus filled his followers with the power of the Holy Spirit (Acts 2 v 1-13).

From the moment that Christ's followers received the gift of the Holy Spirit, the world was impacted by the surge of divine life that began flowing through them. They had a new power, a new purpose, a new praise, and a new pouring out of love and life that turned them and their world upside down!

When the promised Spirit came and filled every believer (Acts 2 v 3), it was a clear sign that, from then on, everyone who named the name of Jesus would receive God's life-changing, empowering Spirit. The third person of the divine Trinity of God is with and is in each one of us who are in Christ, without exception.

The Spirit is vital to every area of the Christian life. Paul explains that we "are being transformed into [Christ's] image with ever-increasing glory, which comes from the Lord, who is the Spirit" (2 Corinthians 3 v 18). When we are in Christ, we become a new creation (2 Corinthians 5 v 17), and the Holy Spirit transforms us, over time, into the likeness of Christ by growing the fruit of the Spirit in us. Not only that, but the Spirit gives us gifts that God will use as we serve him in the world (1 Corinthians 12 v 12, 17).

The Spirit also gives us the spiritual power that will strengthen our witness for Christ. Among the last recorded words of the resurrected Jesus to his disciples was this promise: "You will receive power when the Holy Spirit comes upon you and you will be my witnesses" (Acts 1 v 8). We need to remember that the word "witness" is not a verb; it is a noun. Jesus is describing who we are called to be. The issue isn't whether we desire to be Jesus' witness but whether we'll be his *faithful* witnesses. We are all witnesses; it's just whether we live that out.

That is why the Holy Spirit's role in evangelism is so important. Because of the Spirit's divine power within us, we can do by the Spirit what we could never do by ourselves. Knowing that God is the power in evangelism sets us free from fear because evangelism is not something we do alone—it is about God and his empowering!

When we ask the Holy Spirit to give us boldness, courage, anointing, and power to share the good news, he will! We do not simply give information when we share the gospel; we need the Spirit's power to give our words meaning and effectiveness. It is not our brilliance or clever arguments that bring people to faith; it is God's Spirit working within us, and he also works in non-Christians by opening spiritually blind eyes, by convicting and convincing them so that they can call Jesus Lord (1 Corinthians 12 v 3). It is the Spirit of God that brings about rebirth and produces transformed lives (John 3 v 5-8). We do not have that power, but the Spirit of God does. We are the instruments that God uses, but we are not the agents of transformation.

THE WESTERN CHURCH'S PROBLEM

Yet our lack of dependence on the Spirit's power is perhaps the single most glaring deficiency in the modern Western church, especially when compared to the early church or today in the Global South. The early church demonstrated great courage in their witness and were bursting at the seams with spiritual power, even while they were experiencing catastrophic consequences for proclaiming the gospel. We, on the other hand, often shrink back at merely a raised eyebrow.

Why does the Western church today seem so spiritually anemic by contrast with the early church? Because the early church understood something that we must learn afresh: that God's supernatural power is available to us—that the living God speaks and acts, and that his power, through his Spirit and his word, is able to make all things new in a way that transcends human categories. To live as Christ's witnesses in the 21st century, it is critical that we embrace the power of the Spirit, who resides in us. Yet, as author Fleming Rutledge astutely points out, our essential problem today can be identified in the words which the Lord spoke to a group of Sadducees: "Are you not in error because you do not know the Scriptures or the power of God?" (Mark 12 v 24) (virtueonline.org/what-exactly-gospel-part-ii-fleming-rutledge, accessed 12/23/19).

So, how do we begin not just to understand the power of God's Spirit in theory but to experience it in practice? First, we need to recognize the tremendous difference between the biblical view of reality and our culture's view of reality.

All of Scripture is alive with the vibrant awareness of the supernatural presence of God. The ancient Hebrew writers referred to God as the "living God" (Deuteronomy 5 v 26; 1 Samuel 17 v 26; Joshua 3 v 10; Jeremiah 10 v 10). He is a God who is dynamic and alive. He speaks and he acts. What distinguished Israel from all the other nations on earth is that the very presence of this God dwelled in their midst!

So there is more to see than what we can physically see. When a servant of the prophet Elisha came to him in a state of panic because he had seen enemy armies surrounding the city, Elisha prayed, "Open his eyes, Lord, so that he may see." We are told that "the Lord opened the servant's eyes, and he looked and saw the hills full of horses and chariots of fire all round Elisha" (2 Kings 6 v 16-17). That is how real God's normally unseen presence was to Elisha. To the ancient Hebrews, the "Unseen Real"—the presence of God—was a breath away, and more real and more powerful than even an invading army!

The power of the Spirit is still more evident in the New Testament. As Jesus begins his ministry and declares that he is the long-awaited Messiah, he says, "The Spirit of the Lord is upon me" (Luke 4 v 18-21). Jesus didn't just preach the good news through the power of the Spirit; he demonstrated it through the miracles he performed. Likewise, the Holy Spirit empowered the early church to preach the word of God with courage, anointing, and power; and through the Spirit's power they were able to perform signs and wonders.

FROM SUPERNATURAL TO SECULAR
The biblical view of reality embraces both the seen and the unseen. What is seen is only part of the world, but the unseen

reality—the supernatural presence of God, the Holy Spirit, angels, and demons—is viewed as even more real!

By contrast, in our present culture what is unseen is considered unreal and irrelevant. For something to be considered a part of the real world, we must be able to see, hear, touch, smell, weigh, and measure it. As Os Guinness writes:

> "Advanced modernity tends to make people lose an entire dimension of reality in the name of realism. It reinforces the naturalistic worldview of scientism and the secularist and renders meaningless the supernatural worldview of the Christian." (*Impossible People*, page 23)

In other words, living in our post-Christian culture has negatively impacted believers so that we have difficulty with invisible realities.

Our task as Christians is to recognize and resist the distortions of advanced modernity and to live our lives in light of the unseen world, even while living in a culture that denies that such a thing is possible. We are to "live by faith, not by sight" (2 Corinthians 5 v 7). The difficulty today, as Guinness points out, is that often the unseen is no more real for Christians than it is for skeptics. Too often we behave, without realizing it, as functional atheists.

What do we do to develop a deeper awareness of spiritual realities? We must take seriously the apostle Paul's exhortation to "fix our eyes not on what is seen, but what is unseen" (2 Corinthians 4 v 18). How do we fix on our eyes on the unseen? By learning how to walk in the power of the Spirit, which will reshape our lives and deeply impact our evangelism.

WALKING IN THE SPIRIT

There are several things that will help us to walk in the Spirit, such as abiding in Christ, prayer, and the word of God. We'll look at the first two in this chapter, and at the power of God's word later on.

In John 15, on the night before he was crucified, Jesus told his disciples that he was about to die and would no longer be physically present with them on earth. They were not to despair, however, because he would send the Holy Spirit when he returned to heaven. Through the Spirit, Jesus said, he would remain close to them (and would do the same for all believers from that point on).

Jesus tells his friends that the way to live as Christians is to "dwell in me as I dwell in you" (John 15 v 4, Amplified Bible). We need to remember what he told us: "I am the vine; you are the branches … apart from me you can do nothing" (v 5).

The late author, Leanne Payne, wrote that to walk in the Spirit is learning how to abide in Christ; and to abide in Christ…

> "… is simply the discipline of calling to mind the truth that God is with us and his Spirit dwells within us. When we consistently do this, the miracle of seeing by faith is given." (*The Healing Presence*, page 26)

Payne, in her books and conferences, continually stressed the importance of acknowledging (throughout the day and moment by moment) this one tremendous fact: *There is another who dwells within me.*

As Christians we are not alone, no matter what we feel and whatever our circumstances. We do not wait for the sensation of God's presence. The sense of God's presence is an added gift that we may ask for, and we are grateful when it comes. Walking in the Spirit, or abiding in Christ, simply means that we walk by faith, not feelings. We trust Jesus' words: "I am with you always, even until the end of the age" (Matthew 28 v 20).

Calling to mind that there is another who dwells within me has made a tremendous difference in my life. As a young believer I would have morning devotions, offer spot prayers during the day, and then pray as I lay my head on my pillow at night. But my spiritual life grew by leaps and bounds when I began to understand how to walk in the Spirit.

FOUR WAYS TO ABIDE IN CHRIST

There are four things I started to do that helped me to develop the habit of abiding in Christ:

Remember

I began reminding myself throughout the day and in every situation that I was not alone: that Jesus' presence, through the Spirit, dwelled within me. It is so simple a practice, yet it has made a deep difference in my life. Just consciously acknowledging God's presence reminded me that I no longer needed to rely only on my abilities, nor was I limited by own inadequacies, because the Spirit of God would give me what I lacked from the vast riches of Christ.

Rejoice

I thanked God that his presence was in me and with me, and that I had access to God's power and wisdom and love by my faith in Jesus. Faith includes trusting that Jesus is always with us through his Spirit, so I asked God to increase my faith and to help me learn how to walk by faith.

Request

I asked for God's help throughout the day by praying, "Come, Holy Spirit, come!" If I was speaking to a skeptic, I might ask for the mind of Christ and his wisdom to help me; or for the love of Christ to flow through me to that person; or for the power of God to help extend God's healing; or for boldness and clarity as I shared the gospel. I learned very quickly that if I tried to love others through my own natural compassion, I would run out fast (especially if the person was difficult!) But when I asked to be filled with the love of Jesus, I found that Jesus' love seemed to touch others even when I was least aware of it.

Renew

I daily renewed my commitment to keep in step with the Spirit by opposing my inclination to fall back into self-reliance and self-rule.

There is something very powerful about learning to abide in Christ and drawing upon his resources. It is much more than mere intellectual assent. It's remembering that his Spirit is in us and available to us. To abide in Christ—to "practice the presence of Jesus" as some Christians call it—is a habit that requires daily spiritual discipline. It doesn't come automatically and will take time to master. As Oswald Chambers said, "In the initial stages it is a continual effort until it becomes so much the law of life that you abide in him unconsciously" (*My Utmost for His Highest*, entry for June 14th).

C.S. Lewis wrote:

> "The real problem of the Christian life comes where people do not usually look for it. It comes the very moment you wake up each morning. All your wishes and hopes for the day rush at you like wild animals. And the first

job each morning consists in shoving them all back; in listening to that other voice, taking that other point of view, letting that other larger, stronger, quieter life come flowing in. And so on, all day … We can do it only for moments at first. But from those moments the new sort of life will be spreading through our systems because now we are letting him work at the right part of us."

(*Mere Christianity*, pages 168, 169)

OPEN MY EYES

Another spiritual practice that helps us to walk in the power of the Spirit is prayer. We pray for our skeptic friends and, when appropriate, we pray with them.

When Jesus tells us to follow him, he is inviting us to join him in the redemptive work he is already engaged in! That is why prayer is so important in evangelism. We must ask God, "Where are you already at work in my world, Lord? Who are the people in my life that you are seeking? Open my eyes to see!"

And he will.

A few years ago, Dick and I were invited by a French Christian leader, Raphael Anzenberger, to give evangelism-training conferences to churches in five major cities in France. It was a remarkable time of ministry. Recently, Raphael invited us to come back to do the same thing for churches in the south of France. On the day we arrived in France we met with Raphael to pray for our four conferences in Provence—and we also asked God to guide us personally to the people he was seeking.

A week later, Raphael ordered an Uber to take him and two other pastors to our conference. As they passed a beautiful church building, Raphael asked the driver if he knew the name of the church. The driver said, "It's funny you would ask me that because, when I passed that church last Sunday, I felt an irresistible urge to go inside. So I turned the car around and went in."

Raphael said, "What drew you to go inside?"

"Well, lately I've been feeling an inner emptiness that I can't quite put into words," said the driver. "I've never been a church-goer so I sat way in the back. But during the service I felt this amazing peace come over me. It was like my emptiness was being met by something I can't describe. I wondered if it might be God, but now I'm thinking it was just my imagination."

Raphael said, "No, it wasn't your imagination; you were experiencing the presence of God."

"But how do you know that?" the Uber driver asked. Raphael answered, "Because all three of us are ministers. And like you, I wasn't sure if God was real. So I investigated the Christian faith, and eventually I gave my life to Jesus. All three of us have very different stories, but we can tell you that Jesus has made all the difference in our lives."

Then Raphael said, "So tell me, what do you think is the likelihood that you were in church last Sunday wondering if God is real—and he sends you three ministers to verify it!"

And the driver said, "Ok, prove to me that you guys are really ministers!" Two of the men had their clerical collars on so they unzipped their jackets. And the driver answered, "Wow, I wasn't expecting that! Look, I have a lot of spiritual questions, so could I pull the car over so I can talk to you about them?"

They said yes, and listened carefully to his questions and answered them in a way that seemed to satisfy him. Then Raphael said, "May we pray for you? I want to ask God to reveal to you that Jesus is real."

The Uber driver said, "Yes, I would appreciate that. But first, I need to tell you something. My mother recently became a Christian. After going to church last Sunday, she emailed me on Monday saying she had prayed all week that I would be drawn to go to church. And I was! I keep asking myself if her prayers were the reason why I felt so compelled to go into that church. I've tried to convince myself that it was just a coincidence, and that I hadn't experienced the presence of God at that church. But now, four days later, I pick up three ministers who tell me that it was God in both cases! So yes, please pray for me!"

All four of them prayed together in the cab. Afterwards the pastors gave the driver some material to read, and the pastor who lived the closest to him took down his personal information in order to get in touch and invite him for a meal and to his church.

EXPECT MUCH

Learning to walk in the Spirit means asking the Holy Spirit to guide us to people that he is seeking—and then expecting that he will and being ready when he does. The truth is, expectation is rooted in faith, and it is very important for evangelistic fruitfulness. If we expect little from the Lord, we will often get little. If we expect much, we will ask much, and often we will receive more than we asked or even imagined!

Before an evangelistic outreach or when I am training believers in personal evangelism, I have often asked Christians if they are confident that the Lord will bring some people to faith in Christ. Usually only a few hands go up. Often it is because many have not seen someone become a Christian, so they expect very little. Sadly, this is true not only of lay people but sometimes even of clergy.

Raphael said, "Becky, because we had prayed that first day and specifically asked God to bring into our lives people that he was seeking, I was not surprised it happened. I expected it!"

Without question, our culture poses unique challenges for us, just as the faithful who have gone before us have had to overcome the challenges of their time. That is why God has given us his divine resources to strengthen us in our witness.

Learning to lean upon the Spirit isn't the only thing you and I need to do if we are to be effective witnesses. We also need to share the wonder of the gospel; and we will do that as we grow in (or regain) our excitement about and confidence in that marvelous story—which is the subject of the next section of this book. But here is the foundation of staying salt: apart from him, we can do nothing of any eternal significance; with him, we can do what God desires and our world still so needs—we can speak of Jesus.

QUESTIONS FOR REFLECTION

- "There is more to see than what we can physically see." Why is this so easy to forget? What difference does it make to you to remember that there is a spiritual realm and that God is "a breath away"?
- How can you make it a habit to Remember... Rejoice... Request... Renew?
- Are you asking God for opportunities to talk to others about his Son? How could you learn to expect more, and therefore to ask for more?

SECTION TWO:
THE MESSAGE

CHAPTER FIVE

WE HAVE A BETTER STORY

The poet Muriel Rukeyser once said, "The universe is made of stories, not of atoms" (*Out of Silence*, page 135). Stories are how we make sense of the world and our place in it. The question people want an answer to, whether or not they realize it, is: *Is there a story that is big enough to build our lives upon—a story that gives our lives ultimate meaning and purpose?*

The gospel of Jesus Christ is the most glorious, liberating news that has ever graced our weary, battered planet! The good news of Jesus enables us to discover the meaning of our individual stories by helping us understand the big story: the greatest story ever told. The gospel, rooted in historical fact, ushers in a whole new way of understanding God, our human experience (of our neighbors and ourselves), and the world. The mystery and miracle of the gospel, to paraphrase G.K. Chesterton, is that it is the key that fits the lock—it opens our eyes to understanding reality because the gospel is authored by Christ. It explains who God is, who we are, and the meaning and purpose of our lives.

WHAT IS THE GOOD NEWS?

We will never plumb the depths of the wonder of the gospel; there will always be more to be said. But at its simplest, the gospel is the announcement of what God has done in history through the person of Jesus, who came from heaven to earth for everyone who has ever lived and ever will live. It is the surprising movement of God into human history, recorded in the Bible, and culminating in the life, death, and resurrection of Jesus Christ.

Lady Elizabeth Catherwood, the eldest daughter of the renowned 20th-century preacher Dr. Martyn Lloyd Jones, as a student at Oxford University took courses from C.S. Lewis and J.R.R. Tolkien. She told me that she once heard Lewis remark:

> "People today think that being a Christian is having an experience. The experiential is important, but the Christian faith is based on core beliefs that all Christians must understand, and believe, and then communicate to non-Christians: creation, the fall, redemption (through the life, death, and resurrection of Jesus), and new creation (when Christ returns and restores all things)."

Lesslie Newbigin likewise argued that the best way to express the gospel is to see it as a true story: "What is unique about the Bible is the story it tells, with its climax in the story of the incarnation, ministry, death and resurrection of the Son of God. If this story is true, then it is unique and also universal in its implications for all human history" (*The Gospel in a Pluralistic Society*, page 97). In other words, it is the story of how God revealed who he was, first to the people of Israel, and then how God came to earth and revealed himself in human flesh in the person of Jesus. Through the life, death, and resurrection of Jesus Christ, salvation is made available to the world. The scholar and author N.T. Wright puts it this way: "We are inviting people into a whole new way of understanding human experience and God, a whole new way of life rooted in the life, death and resurrection of Jesus" (*Surprised by Hope*, page 11).

Yet the challenge for us today is not only understanding what the gospel is but knowing how to communicate the gospel in the pluralistic West when our cultural landscape is constantly changing. The impact of post-modernity means that communicating the gospel will not be without its challenges. I recently had a conversation with a woman who said, "I believe we must honor the god who dwells within our psyches and trust our hearts to guide us—and Oprah really agrees with me!" Also not long ago, a man told me, "Human beings are nothing more than meaningless pieces of protoplasm: a fortuitous concurrence of atoms. There is no God, as Darwin has so clearly proven."

How do we communicate the gospel in a way that people coming from this kind of viewpoint will understand, and so begin to see the credibility and goodness of? Where do we start? If you are a Christian, you believe that the gospel is true, and true for all; and that it contains the answers to our deepest needs. Nevertheless, a great deal of the Christian message runs counter to our culture, and formulaic presentations of that message will no longer work (if they ever did). We must—and we can—respond winsomely, intelligently, and persuasively to people who have very different views and have never really engaged with the gospel before.

What increases our confidence is that the Christian worldview is based not on what we think about God but on what God has revealed about himself: Christianity is a religion of revelation. God has made himself known in many ways, but his primary revelation is through his written word: the Bible. When we bear witness to our faith, we are not sharing merely our own experience but the experience of God's life-changing revelation to us through Christ.

So for us today, it is absolutely vital that we first understand the "what" of the gospel message, and how it provides the answers for the questions people are asking; or, to put it another way, how its treasures are what people are searching for. In our truth-denying culture we are tempted to lose confidence in the power and the truth of the gospel. If we do not understand what we believe, and how it truly is good news for this world, then we will not be persuasive in communicating our faith to others—and we will not even want to do that.

IT'S BETTER THAN WE THINK

Years ago I began to study theology to help me gain a deeper understanding of the gospel. What I quickly realized is that while the gospel is certainly comprehensible, it is so rich and expansive that even a lifetime of study could not reveal all of its wonders and mysteries. That is why Jesus used so many metaphors and illustrations to explain the kingdom of God, because it cannot be captured in a single idea.

As I was pondering the best way to communicate the gospel, I decided that I would recite the gospel to myself every day. Back then I was a mother of young children, so I spent a lot of time in the car driving the kids to various activities. Whenever I was alone in the car, I would speak the gospel out loud to myself. At first it felt a bit strange, especially seeing the looks of people in the cars next to me! But soon I found myself exhilarated by the wonder of the gospel.

"Skeptics can tell if we are merely reciting a set of beliefs or if we have fallen in love with the One we are proclaiming."

I realized in a fresh way that this is one thing that cannot be faked. Skeptics will try to counter our arguments and our defense of the Christian faith—but they can tell if we are merely reciting a set of beliefs or if we have fallen in love with the One we are proclaiming.

There are three things to keep in mind as we explore the meaning of the gospel. First, the gospel has been described as a multifaceted diamond because its beauty can be understood and experienced in many ways. While the gospel is authored by Jesus Christ (Galatians 1 v 11-12), we still need to pay attention to the context in which we're sharing it. While the essence of the gospel is unchanging, there are many ways to share the gospel story. Paul emphasized different aspects of the gospel depending on who he was speaking to. Knowing whether our skeptic friends have a post-Christian mindset or a more traditional moral perspective will help us know where to start in explaining the gospel.

Second, we don't have to put all the gospel points into one single conversation. Reading Paul's gospel speeches in the book of Acts, it is noteworthy how often he left things out! Whether we have the opportunity to share an abbreviated version of the whole gospel or we discuss only one aspect of the gospel, the point is that we do not have to say everything every time.

Third, the challenge in communicating the gospel is to not dilute the gospel by capitulating to the reigning worldview. For example, the mistake Christians made in the 18th century, in attempting to reach people in their age of rationalism, was to present the gospel as a list of propositional truths that required only intellectual assent. Yet Jesus offered a whole new way of seeing reality and a new way of living. The Gospels reveal converts who became disciples and whose lives were profoundly, radically transformed, because they understood that the gospel impacted every dimension of their lives. Following Christ was not understood merely in individualistic terms that focused only on personal conversion. They understood that the gospel must be lived out in communal and public life as well.

But neither must we present the gospel in a way that offers only a subjective experience of fulfillment: as private and not public truth, as merely our own experience rather than "true truth" for all, as one way among many options. This is a postmodern approach that will not result in disciples who know what is required of them, and the fruit it produces will be weak. While seekers certainly need to know that surrendering their lives to Christ will provide joy and peace, they also need to know that discipleship demands sacrifice and total allegiance because Jesus Christ is Lord.

I frequently hear Christians say these three things:

1. I'm not sure I really understand the gospel message myself.
2. How do I answer the questions that arise when I share the gospel?
3. How is the gospel truly relevant to unbelievers today?

The purpose of this section of the book is to address these very issues by exploring what the Bible teaches about each aspect of the gospel; to look at the pushback we may receive from skeptics, and at how to communicate the relevance and beauty of the gospel while sensitively critiquing their answers yet affirming their longings, so that we can point them towards Christ, the source of and answer for all human fulfillment (see my chapter in *Joyfully Spreading the Word,* pages 21-34).

The evangelistic approach of Blaise Pascal, the brilliant mathematician and theologian of the 1600s, is worth noting:

"Men despise religion. They hate it and are afraid it may be true. The cure for this is first to show that religion is not contrary to reason, but worthy of reverence and respect. Next make it attractive, make good men wish it were true, and then show that it is."

(*Pensées*, page 300)

That may sound intimidating! But it is possible, and it does prove effective. Let's begin where the Bible begins: with the story of creation.

QUESTIONS FOR REFLECTION

- How does it increase your confidence to know that the gospel is not based on your own thoughts but is authored by Jesus Christ?
- In what ways does it free you to know that we don't necessarily have to give the entire gospel in a single conversation?
- "If we do not understand what we believe, and how it truly is good news for this world, then we will not be persuasive in communicating our faith to others—and we will not even want to do that." How excited are you personally about the gospel right now? Why? And what impact can you see that this has on your desire to tell others that gospel?

CHAPTER SIX

CREATION: HOW LIFE WAS MEANT TO BE

"Hey, I might believe in God if only God would give me some clear sign! Like making a large deposit in my name at a Swiss bank." (Woody Allen)

You may have noticed that while people today offer a variety of answers to the meaning of life, the questions haven't really changed much from past generations. Is there a God? Who am I? Why am I here? What is the purpose of life?

You may have also noticed that today's celebrated skeptics are eager to share their thoughts, and particularly their views on the biblical God. The late Christopher Hitchens, the author and atheist whose best-known book was *God Is Not Great: How Religion Poisons Everything*, described the God of the Bible as a "heavenly dictator" and wrote that heaven "would be like living in a celestial North Korea" (*Letters to a Young Contrarian*, page 64). Richard Dawkins, another famous atheist, in his book *The God Delusion*, depicts the God of the Old Testament as a "misogynistic, homophobic, racist, infanticidal, genocidal, filicidal, pestilential, megalomaniacal, sadomasochistic, capriciously malevolent bully" (page 31). If only Dawkins would tell us what he really thinks!

What a contrast their beliefs are to what we actually read in Genesis 1 and 2! God is revealed as our Creator, who created life out of love, delight and pure goodness. The biblical story of creation is presented as a love story from start to finish.

STARTING WITH GOD

In a world where we are presented with multiple-choice starting points, we must start where the Bible starts: "In the beginning God created the heavens and the earth" (Genesis 1 v 1). The creation story tells us a great deal about who God is.

God is eternal: he is before all things and without beginning or end. He has no competitor or peer. He commands, and it is accomplished.

God is the Creator: through him all things came into being, because God is the cause and source of life. God created out of nothing; he needs no help, which means that God is above and beyond all he has made, and distinct from it.

God is good: in Genesis, and throughout the Bible, we see that God's character is righteous and holy, loving and merciful, trustworthy and faithful.

God is personal and communicative: God is not some distant, impersonal power or an energy field. He is a loving, personal God who delights and shows parental, nurturing concern over what he has created.

God created humans as the apex of his entire physical creation and gave his highest accolade to them (Genesis 1 v 31). What made Adam and Eve unique, in contrast with the rest of creation, was that only humans were created in the image of God. The first human beings were given language, creativity, love, holiness, immortality, and freedom (within divine limits) to choose their actions. They were created to love and know God, to live in harmony with him and the rest of creation. God gave (and gives) humanity a purpose: to reveal God to the rest of his creation, and to rule the world as God's stewards under his sovereign, loving rule.

Everything God created was made for God's glory and humanity's benefit. Genesis 1 – 2 tells us that Adam and Eve had a close, intimate relationship with God; a loving relationship with each other; fulfilling work to do; and a world full of pleasures, tastes, sights, and smells. They were created to enjoy God's goodness and submit to God's gracious will.

All of Eden was given to them, with only one restriction: "You are free to eat from any tree in the garden; but you must not eat from the tree of the knowledge of good and evil, for when you eat from it you will certainly die" (Genesis 2 v 16-17). This restriction, as we saw in chapter 2, served as an important protection because it reminded Adam and Eve of the limits of their humanity: they were creatures, not the Creator. It was also a warning of the consequence if they chose independence instead of God-dependence: they would surely die.

This means that human beings are given a choice to accept or reject God's ways. Why is this so important? Because it reveals that God's world is founded on love, on relationship. Our first parents lived in the reality of God's original intention: dwelling in perfect unity and harmony without sin, suffering, and death. When people say, "If God is good, why would he create a world with so much brokenness?" we can point to the fact that this broken world is not the way God designed it.

The principle feature of life—life as God intends—is a lavish gift. The gospel message from start to finish is God's personal offer of amazing grace!

CREATION: HOW THE WORLD SEES IT

What objections do skeptics frequently raise about how life came to be? My purpose here is not to give exhaustive answers but rather to help us get started.

Evolution

Often skeptics want to jump immediately to the subject of evolution: the idea that life began in an evolutionary process. Atheistic evolutionists believe that the theory of evolution and natural selection can explain the universe much better than the idea of an intelligent design carried out by a God.

What I often tell skeptics is that Christians have different views on creation and evolution over issues such as how old the earth is, what Genesis means by the word "day," and to what degree, if any, God chose to use evolution. Christian opinions vary depending on how we interpret Genesis 1 – 3: specifically on what kind of literary genre we think is being used, and how we interpret the early chapters of Genesis in light of the entire biblical revelation.

But this is not what I want to focus on in conversations with unbelievers (or in this chapter!) What non-Christians often ignore is that they cannot definitively answer the "first cause" of creation: how life actually came to be. However we answer that question, we cannot do so based on scientific knowledge. Though they are usually reluctant to admit it, skeptics have a position of faith in this area, just as we do.

Usually if we acknowledge right at the start that sincere Christians have different views on this subject, we don't have to spend much time on the evolution issue, nor is it necessary unless this issue is a deal-breaker for someone. Whether believers come to the view that God completed the job of creation in six literal days or over a much longer period, the heart of the matter is that God is the Creator of all things. That is the biblical focus, and it needs to be our focus as well.

Science and Christianity

Another topic often raised is the assumed belief that there is a clash between science and Christianity. While, at times, there appears to be a conflict between science and faith, there is less evidence to support that view than skeptics may think. In fact, science as a field of study actually began as a result of the Protestant faith! Furthermore, there are many scientists today who are deeply committed Christians. The Oxford don, mathematician, and devout Christian John Lennox, who famously debated atheist Richard Dawkins, has written extensively on how science and faith do not clash (for instance, in *Can Science Explain Everything?*). It is fair to say that many people have taken it on trust that science has undermined or disproved religion—though they've never really thought about whether it's true.

Reality Is Only What We Can Measure

There are some who scoff at the notion that there is an unseen reality behind what we can see. In other words, they are "materialists," who view reality as only what they can see, hear, touch, smell, weigh, measure, and calculate. They believe that creation began as an accident and out of that accident life came into being.

Therefore, since life is an accident and there is no God, life has no meaning.

The question is, can they live consistently by their belief that life has no meaning and human beings have no intrinsic worth? In their deepest heart do they really believe that their children and the significant others they cherish are simply meaningless pieces of protoplasm?

"I Am Spiritual but Not Religious"

Sometimes I talk with people who believe there is something beyond what they can see in the natural world. Perhaps they've experienced moments of awe or wonder when looking at a sunset or watching a dramatic storm over a lake.

This view usually looks something like what a New Age devotee once said to me: "I believe we must honor the god who dwells in our nature, remembering that rocks, trees and fruit are as sacred as people." This view is more in line with the view that the world is either identical to God (pantheism) or in every part an expression of God's nature (panentheism). This is, of course, different from the biblical description that says there is a personal God who existed before the world began and who is distinct from creation.

One thing that usually challenges such a view of life is crisis. For example, the New Age devotee that I quoted above, upon learning that she might have cancer, phoned a New Age hotline. The person answering her call told her, "You must look within to find your deity. You are the universe; you are God; you are a rock and a flower." My friend later asked me, "If I am God, then what kind of God gets cancer? [She could have added, 'What kind of God is cancer?'] I realized in that moment that I needed a God outside of creation who was powerful; I longed for a personal God who loved me, not some divine impersonal energy." It was this experience that eventually led her to place her faith in Christ.

WHY CREATION IS SUCH GOOD NEWS

How do we communicate the relevance of the creation story in a way that shows it truly is good news? First, we need to share, unhesitatingly, our joy and excitement over who God is!

God is our Creator, who created life out of love, delight, and pure goodness! The creation account is an incredible love story where we see God expressing joy and wonder over his creation, like an artist delighting in his masterpiece. That is a far more compelling narrative than the arid secular one that says the world is the result of a violent, cataclysmic accident.

Creation is good: not only is the creation story magnificent and moving, but it also provides a logical foundation and explanation for how to understand reality. In Genesis, God created the world and declared it good. God didn't say the earth was evil or worthless; neither did he say it was divine and to be worshiped. The implications of this are massive. The creation story provides the reason for why we care for the earth and must never abuse it. It also shows us that we are not to mistakenly worship nature or objects, but rather the God who created all things!

Creation is God's work: God created human life and called it "very good." All human life is precious to God and every human being bears God's image. That is why we are to treat human beings with dignity, respect, and love. It is why, for instance, we view racism as evil. The creation story also tells us that human beings were created to live in peace and harmony, not strife and chaos. The meaning of life, from the biblical perspective, is not about power but about love—not about transactions but about relationships. That is quite different from the modern secular narrative.

One way to communicate the relevance of the creation story to skeptics is to point to the evidence of our God-imprinted natures.

Our Concern for Justice, Equality, and Human Rights

One of the remarkable aspects of the creation narrative is that it makes sense of what most non-Christians already (at least to some extent) believe: that all lives matter! The secular narrative tells us that life is meaningless, so how can an atheist logically explain why human life must be valued? The creation story, on the other hand, provides the reason why we feel passionate about justice, fairness, and racial equality—it's because we are made in God's image. The Creator God is a righteous God who loves his creation and who stands firmly opposed to all forms of injustice, and he made us to have the same attitude.

Our Response to Beauty

When we read of the beauty in paradise in Genesis 1 – 2, we see that God is the source of beauty and he created human beings to recognize and respond to beauty, as well. For example, the first recorded poem in the Bible is when God introduced Adam to Eve. Adam was overcome with wonder and awe: 'This is now bone of my bones and flesh of my flesh…" (Genesis 2 v 23).

Once again, the challenge for skeptics is how to explain their response of wonder when it goes against their secular worldview: that there is no ultimate meaning in life. An atheist friend of mine, after giving birth to her first child, said, "Becky, giving birth to my son felt... miraculous. Yet women have been giving birth since the beginning of time. So why am I so overwhelmed with wonder when I look into the eyes of my baby? How do I explain this sense of awe, especially when I am an atheist?"

What is wonder? Webster's Dictionary defines "wonder" as "the emotion aroused by something awe-inspiring, astounding or marvelous. An event that is inexplicable by the laws of nature." The late renowned sociologist Peter Berger captured this idea of wonder when he wrote of "signals of transcendence." According to Berger, "these are phenomena that are to be found within the domain of our 'natural' reality but appear to point beyond that reality" (*A Rumor of Angels*, page 53). So, as Os Guinness writes, "Our privilege as Christians and apologists, by our lives as well as our words, is to help people to hear, to listen and to understand those signals, and then to help them follow to where they lead" (*Fool's Talk*, page 147). If we follow the logic of that signal, they actually move us towards faith in God.

When G.K. Chesterton came to London to study at Slade School of Fine Art, he was a convinced atheist. Everywhere he looked, he saw evidence that the world was broken and dark. What broke into his worldview of darkness and pessimism? The wonder of the beauty of a dandelion! It was Chesterton's experience of wonder in encountering beauty that caused him to re-evaluate his atheism, and this became the catalyst that led him to become a devoted follower of Christ.

But wonder is a notion that is somewhat out of fashion at present, as the author Flannery O'Connor points out:

> "We moderns are embarrassed by wonder—because wonder suggests mystery. Moderns aren't comfortable

with anything we can't control or dominate or explain away." (*Mystery and Manners,* page 123)

That is why prayer is so important: we must ask God to show us what might cause our skeptic friends to start to respond in wonder. It's also why asking good questions is so important, because they can gently help our friends to question their own skepticism, which may lead them to reconsider their own beliefs and become curious about what we believe.

I came to know an Eastern European woman who was raised in a communist country by parents who were brilliant academics and fervent atheists. She too was an atheist and a gifted violinist. We began having spiritual conversations, but they never seemed to go anywhere—until the day I asked her this question: "I'm curious. Is there anything that has ever caused you to doubt your atheism?"

She thought for a moment and then answered, "Just one thing: when I play glorious, beautiful music, like a Bach composition. Sometimes, as I play, I become so caught up that it almost feels like I am worshiping. I am transported to some other place, and I think to myself, 'I am not just a physical being with biological drives. There must be more to life than what I can see.' But I know that sounds crazy."

"Actually," I replied, "I think your response is very revealing. As a musician, you probably know that Johann Sebastian Bach was a deeply committed Christian. It's why he wrote *Soli Deo Gloria* on every piece of music he wrote: *To the glory of God alone.* Bach believed that writing and performing his music was an act of worship to God. So what you need to figure out is why your head believes one thing but your heart is saying something completely different. They both can't be right, so which of your responses is closer to what is real and true?"

"Actually, I wish there was a God," she said. "But even if God exists, I am certain God is certainly not interested in me or the greatest passion of my life—my music."

I said, "Did you know there are biblical descriptions of heaven that describe a place where there is glorious music and singing and worship? Which suggests that music existed before the earth was created. I believe your love for music comes from the One who created music—God himself!"

Several months later I invited her, along with other skeptic friends, to a Bible study looking at Jesus, and she came. What was the Bible story that moved her to tears? The story of the shepherds in Luke 2, who are watching their flocks at night when suddenly the heavens open up, an angel speaks, and there is glorious angelic praise!

Though it's not entirely clear whether the angels sang or spoke their praise that first Christmas night, my friend was gripped. She asked where in the Bible it described music and singing in heaven. Because of our previous conversation, I had looked up other verses, just in case she asked! So I read aloud how God describes what happened when he created the world: "the morning stars sang together and all the angels shouted for joy" (Job 38 v 7-8). I read Zephaniah 3 v 17, explaining that this was a picture of when Christ returns to earth at the end of history and after the final judgment, when all believers are reunited with Christ: "He will take great delight in you, he will quiet you with his love, and he will rejoice over you with singing."

Tears sprung to her eyes again, and she said, "God himself sings? It's almost too beautiful to bear!" Here is what had caused her to take Jesus' claims seriously: the reality that music is created and singing is something God does. In our evangelism we need to answer the rational questions of the mind, but we also need to show how the gospel answers our hearts as well. The gospel addresses the whole person, and so must we.

It was having a baby that caused my atheist friend to wonder if there was more to life. It was playing Bach that caused my violinist friend to experience awe and to question if God might exist. Never forget that these experiences of wonder are there to point us to another reality—to a deeper reality: to the One we have been searching for, perhaps unaware, all along.

That is why we need to ask our non-Christian friends if they have ever had an experience so profound that it caused them, even momentarily, to wonder if God exists? Many people answer yes to that question. Some say they think they have once experienced God's presence. These experiences are the beeping "signals of transcendence," and our task is to try to make people more aware of their human longings and desires, and what their passions point to.

After the last Bible study my violinist friend said, "Becky, when I discovered you were a Christian, I was determined that we'd never be friends. I loathed religion and felt believers were intellectual morons. I used every opportunity to say mocking things about Christians in your presence. What I couldn't understand was why you didn't avoid me. In fact, you actually seemed to like me."

She went on: "As our relationship grew, I saw that your faith wasn't mindless. You took my questions seriously, but you also asked questions that challenged my own beliefs and really made me think. Yet I wouldn't have attended the Bible study if we hadn't first established a friendship."

Then she added, "No one is more surprised than I am to find myself so drawn to Jesus. The truth is, I'm not the same woman I was when we first met. Many of my prejudices about Christians have subsided, and I am realizing that there are intelligent answers to some of my objections to faith. I still have doubts, and I'm not ready to become a Christian—but I definitely want to keep exploring Christianity. Could we do another Bible study?"

To see someone move from deep hostility to wanting to continue exploring Christianity is a cause for rejoicing! When she saw that the biblical story of a Creator God explained her powerful response to the beauty of music, she became increasingly open and started to take Jesus seriously.

Creation is the opening act of the gospel story. And it is beautiful. So the obvious question is: how did we get from paradise to our present mess? No one doubts that our planet is in serious trouble. The challenge for all of us is how to explain the mess we are in—which is the topic of our next chapter.

QUESTIONS FOR REFLECTION

- What truths about God and his creation in this chapter have most excited you?
- Which of the common objections discussed here do you come across most often? How would you answer these objections?
- As you think about how to communicate the relevance of the creation account to skeptics, what aspect of that story has most struck you? Justice, beauty, wonder? Something else?

CHAPTER SEVEN

THE FALL: WHAT'S WRONG WITH THE WORLD

"I find it amazing that moderns reject the doctrine of original sin when it is the only Christian doctrine that can be empirically verified." (G.K. Chesterton)

Chesterton, the 20th century wit, author and Catholic thinker, once replied to a letter printed in a newspaper that was entitled "What's Wrong with the World." In his response, which was also printed in the newspaper, he wrote:

"The answer to the question, 'What is Wrong?' is, or should be, 'I am wrong.' Until a man can give that answer his idealism is only a hobby."

(*Chesterton at the Daily News*, volume 3)

Chesterton believed that the core problem of the universe could be stated in two words: I am. Likewise, the Russian novelist, Aleksandr Solzhenitsyn, in his book *The Gulag Archipelago*, said that the lesson he learned in prison camp (that ultimately led to his conversion to Christianity) was that the line between good and evil runs through each person (*The Gulag Archipelago*, part one, page 168). The Bible sums it up in one word: sin.

Yet for all the evidence of evil around us, the notion of sin is seriously out of favor. In our post-Christian culture, people find the idea of sin outrageous or, at best, hopelessly old-fashioned. So here is our challenge as Christians: *how do we talk about sin?*

Let's start in the place where everyone agrees: something has gone wrong in this world and must be made right. We see the wrong in world wars, racism, environmental problems, genocides, terrorism, human trafficking, exploitation of children—and in our own personal battles: broken relationships, anger, greed, addictions, and so on. Yet the world remains puzzled and lacks a coherent explanation as to why our planet is such a mess.

It has not always been this way. For centuries it was understood that sin, in all its forms, was the ultimate source of human misery. It's only since the time of the Enlightenment in the 18th century that we have seen the concept of sin fade away as a category for understanding the human condition. The truth is, few concepts have less cash value today than sin. Our culture uses new names for what ails us: low self-esteem, neurosis, addiction, psychological wounding, and so on. It isn't that these issues are not a reality; it is that such analysis does not go anywhere near deep enough to reveal the root cause.

We are struggling with the symptoms of an age-old disease that we have lost the capacity to diagnose. That is why the biblical doctrine of sin is more relevant today than ever. It is what prompted Ernest Becker, the atheist and social psychologist, to write: "The plight of moderns is that they are sinners with no word for it" (*The Denial of Death*, page 164).

THE REASON FOR THE WRONGNESS

The Bible makes clear that all the wrongs we see around us, and in us, can be traced back to the time when the first human beings rebelled against God. Genesis 3 looks squarely at good and evil and tells us what happened that caused our planet to go from the paradise described in chapters 1 – 2 to our present brokenness.

In Genesis 3 we read that Adam and Eve rejected God's rule; they disobeyed God's command and chose to be self-ruled. This was sin entering humanity. There is now no area of human personhood that is not infected by sin—even though we still (albeit imperfectly) reflect the image of God in which each human being is made. We are beautiful but broken—made, but marred. The perfection that God had established was broken, and human beings have been in the grip of sin ever since. As Paul says, "All have sinned and fall short of the glory of God" (Romans 3 v 23).

The Essence of Sin

A psychiatrist friend once described to me the typical problems that drove people to seek her help. Then she stopped and said, with a note of skepticism, "Ah, but you're a Christian, so you think the problem is that we're all sinners." I asked how she thought the Bible defined sin, and with a wry smile she answered, "Oh, probably something along the lines of drugs, sex, and rock-n-roll?"

"But that's behavior," I said. "From the biblical perspective, sin at its core isn't just misdeeds. Bad behavior is the result of sin, not the cause."

"Ok," she said, "I'll bite. What is the root cause of sin?"

She asked exactly the right question—but how could I answer in a way that was faithful and that she would understand? After all, in any discussion of sin, we tend to lose our audience very quickly!

Having a God Complex

One way to describe sin is to explain that we have a God complex: we keep getting ourselves and God mixed up (see Richard F. Lovelace, *Dynamics of Spiritual Life*). The problem isn't a psychological complex; it's a spiritual complex! Instead of having faith in God, we have faith in ourselves, and we live as if we are in charge. Sin is the deliberate refusal to believe in and worship God as God, and it is the prideful claim of the right to run our own lives.

Therefore, instead of accepting our creaturely dependence upon our loving Creator, we insist on our autonomy. We think being self-governed is what sets us free when, in fact, it only leads to confusion and bondage. As C.S. Lewis wrote, "Fallen man is not simply an imperfect creature who needs improvement; he is a rebel who must lay down his arms" (*Mere Christianity*, page 50).

Worshiping the Wrong Thing

Here is another aspect to sin. Paul writes that if we do not worship God, we will worship something else—a God-substitute: "They exchanged the truth about God for a lie and worshiped and served the creature rather than the Creator" (Romans 1 v 25). We seek to find meaning, purpose, and identity by depending on things other than God. These could be good things or bad things, but whatever we use as our God-substitute the Bible calls an idol. Instead of treasuring and loving God above all else, we rebel against God by depending on something else, and therefore we end up worshiping created things—be it a person, a possession, a position, or anything else—instead of God.

Sin's Outcome

When Adam and Eve turned away from God in rebellion, God declared his righteous judgment, just as he had promised he would. Suffering and death fell upon the human race. The consequence of Adam and Eve's rebellion was disastrous: the human race became catastrophically separated from God. The perfect trust and warm intimate friendship they had enjoyed with God and with each other were destroyed. Adam and Eve were removed from the immediate presence of God, and they experienced a spiritual separation from God they had never previously known. In short, sin and its consequences impacted every aspect of their lives.

Because of sin, we are now living on a planet in a profound state of dysfunction. All the brokenness on our planet, both without and within, is ultimately the consequence of not allowing God to be God. The problem is not the result of a design problem within God's nature. The core of the issue is a spiritual problem: human beings have rebelled against God. The consequence of the issue is a moral problem: human beings, in rebellion against God, now make our own rules, and in doing so hurt ourselves and those around us.

Nevertheless, God didn't stop loving Adam and Eve when they rebelled, and so we see God tenderly making them better clothes than they had made for themselves, to protect them once they were outside the garden. What Genesis 3 v 14-15 reveals is that before the beginning of time and the human revolt, the triune God had already decided on his plan of how to rescue the planet once humans had turned from him: God would send his Son, the Messiah (Titus 1 v 2). He did not come to help us be good; he came to rescue us. As Ravi Zacharias describes it so well:

"The story of the 'fall' enables us to be honestly realistic and tremendously hopeful at the same time."

"The Christian faith, simply stated, reminds us that our fundamental problem is not moral; rather, our fundamental problem is spiritual ... a moral life alone cannot bridge what separates us from God. Herein lies the cardinal difference between the moralizing religions and Jesus' offer to us. Jesus does not offer to make bad people good but to make dead people alive."

(*The Grand Weaver*, page 82)

The story of the "fall" enables us to be honestly realistic and tremendously hopeful at the same time. Even in the story of human rebellion, there is hope and not despair because we see the promise of God's grace.

SIN: HOW THE WORLD SEES IT

Over the years I have had countless conversations with unbelievers about faith. At some point I usually ask, "What do you believe is the biggest problem in the world, and what do you believe is the solution?" Their answers vary depending on their age, life experience, cultural background and worldview. Here are some responses that we may hear that indicate how people see the problem:

Human Beings Are Good: Let's Focus on the Positive

Not long ago, I was seated at a dinner party next to one of the top political leaders from a European country. During our conversation he said he believed in the essential goodness of human nature. I said that, as a Christian, what I appreciated about the biblical worldview was its realism: all human beings are made in the image of God and have immense worth and value, but we are also flawed due to sin. "That seems to fit the facts of reality as I look at the world and into my own heart," I said.

He replied, "Well, I don't see people as sinners. I believe we have been given the gift of reason—and through reason we can resolve our deepest differences." We had a lively and enjoyable conversation about our differing opinions. Towards the end of dessert I said, "Do you know what teensy weensy bit of evidence suggests that the biblical understanding of human nature is the accurate one?" He smiled and said, "Ok, try me. Where's the evidence?" "How about all of human history?!" I answered. He laughed and said, "Point taken!"

The lesson here is that we can have a positive conversation about faith with someone with very different views, and even defend a biblical view without being aggressive or overbearing. With a light touch and even humor it's possible to stimulate someone's curiosity about the Christian faith.

In my experience, people identify the source of human troubles either as an internal problem (envy, greed, addiction, low self-esteem) or as an external problem (poverty, racism, sexism).

My Problems Are Internal

I once met a famous race-car driver who told me that in his racing days he felt that he had it all: fame, money, and women (I tell part of this story in my book *Out of the Saltshaker*). When that began to feel empty, he started engaging in reckless behavior. Then he had a near-fatal car accident that ended his career. In his despair he became a full-fledged alcoholic.

Eventually Rick joined Alcoholics Anonymous, and when we met he had been sober for sixteen months. He talked at length about his journey, his gratitude for being sober, and the profound regrets and shame he was still wrestling with.

I said, "You know, Rick, the pain of facing your regrets is really tough. But I can't tell you how much I admire your courage in facing yourself, owning your problem, and sticking with your recovery. I think acknowledging our problems is the hardest work any of us can ever do. It's hard on our pride, but ultimately it is liberating, don't you agree?"

"No question about it," he answered. "The hardest part was to stop blaming everybody else and accept responsibility for what was my problem alone. It was so freeing to finally own it. Becky, you really seem to understand, and you don't feel judgmental. Hey, are you in recovery too?"

"Yes, I am in recovery," I said. "But not for alcohol. I'm in recovery for a problem far deeper than alcoholism."

"Would you mind sharing what your problem is?" Rick asked, as his eyes widened.

I said, "I'm in recovery for what the Bible calls sin. You know why I don't seem judgmental to you? Because I've learned that the only thing that separates people are their symptoms—but we all suffer from the same underlying disease of sin."

"I don't think I get it," he said. "What's the difference between being a drunk and being a sinner? Isn't it the same thing?"

"Alcoholism is the destructive behavior," I told him. "But the real culprit is what lurks behind the behavior. The core of sin isn't just a set of behaviors. You could never drink a drop of alcohol again, Rick, and still insist on running your own life rather than letting God be in charge. Our destructive behavior, in whatever form it takes, is always the inevitable result of refusing to let God be God."

"Oh, man, I can really identify with what you're saying," he said. "No one could tell me what to do, and look where it got me. But if AA is the treatment for alcoholism, then what's the treatment for sin?"

"Rick, you told me that you once felt like you had it all, but it didn't satisfy," I answered. "Then you became an alcoholic, and now you have achieved sobriety, but you still feel something is missing in your life. You said that since joining AA you've been trying to discover the name of this higher power. Rick, I know the name: his name is Jesus. And the treatment for sin is that Jesus, God's Son, died on the cross. All of us have tried to live our lives as if we are God, and look at the mess we've created! We all deserve God's judgment, but Jesus stepped in and took it for us. He rose from the dead and offers to heal our brokenness, to forgive our sins, and to make us whole. What Jesus offers isn't just recovery but transformation!"

"But how is that even possible? And anyway, your sins couldn't possibly be as bad as mine!" he said.

From there, I explained to Rick how Jesus had died on the cross to offer everyone salvation—including him. Rick was a strong, rough-hewn kind of guy, but upon hearing the gospel of grace, tears began streaming down his cheeks, and he committed his life to Christ.

There were many moments in that conversation where I could have lost Rick (and where I have lost others in discussions about the nature of sin). Reflecting on our conversation, I was struck by three key things we need to do in order to address the difficult topic of sin without alienating people.

First, we need to express love and compassion, and avoid being self-righteous or judgmental. After all, we also have been saved by grace, not by being good or by sinning less! We must not present ourselves as finished products. Our message is not that we are perfect but that we know the One who is perfect, and day by day we are receiving divine forgiveness and divine help to become conformed to Christ's image. As D.T. Niles, a Sri Lankan pastor and evangelist who died in 1970, once memorably said, "Evangelism is one beggar telling another beggar where to get food."

Second, we need to thank people for their courage in sharing their stories with us, while encouraging them to take a deeper look. We need to help them to identify the longings and aspirations that lie behind their struggles. When success and fame didn't satisfy Rick, he used alcohol to drown out his inner emptiness. Even after achieving sobriety, Rich was still looking for meaning and for relief from his shame and guilt. We show people that their human longings aren't there to mock them. They are important clues that will help them see who they are and why they need God. What Rick hadn't realized was that he needed God's love and forgiveness to be set free.

Third, when people are spiritually open, we have the opportunity to explain why sin is the deepest problem that we all share. They are not alone. But we must talk honestly and clearly about sin—in language that they can understand.

The Problem Is External

Many people, conversely, believe the source of the human crisis to be an external problem, not so much "in here" as "out there." It's the view behind the maxim of the 18th-century philosopher Jean-Jacques Rousseau: "Man is born free, and everywhere he is in chains," meaning that we're born good and noble, but the world corrupts us. So, the thinking goes, solve the outside problem and we solve the human condition.

As Christians we readily agree that any form of injustice that oppresses people is evil. The biblical prophets railed against injustice, and they called God's people to do something about it—and promised that God would bring judgment for it (see, for example, Amos 2 v 6-8; Micah 2 v 1-4; 6 v 8). Our Christian witness (personally and corporately through the church) will suffer a tremendous credibility problem if the world does not see the evidence of God's compassion working through us.

But, as Martyn Lloyd Jones reminds us, "Justice without justification is always inadequate." In other words, as important as it is to work on overcoming the massive social problems of our day, there is a deeper problem still. Even if we could solve the social problems, we would still have a heart problem because we are separated from God due to our sin.

Unless Christians address the seriousness of sin in all its forms, our witness will lack spiritual power. Back in 2010, at the Lausanne Convention for World Evangelism in Cape Town, I led the track on personal evangelism. I invited the Nigerian Archbishop, Benjamin Kwashi, and Michael Ramsden, now President of RZIM (Ravi Zacharias International Ministries) to join me. Each of us taught several sessions: Ramsden spoke on how to communicate gospel truth to those living in a post-truth culture; I spoke on how to communicate faith from a global perspective; Archbishop Kwashi spoke on how the gospel addresses the problem of evil on both individual and systemic levels. He said, "Africans have been dealing with injustice for a very long time. We are grateful for the passion for justice that we are seeing in our Western brothers and sisters, especially in the young."

He went on:

"What puzzles us, however, is your hesitancy to also address personal sin and the need for repentance in order to be restored to God through Christ. I understand your fear of reducing the gospel to only a privatized, individualistic understanding of conversion. Yet, the turning point in all human history is that Jesus was crucified, died and was buried, and arose from the dead for the transformation of the human heart *and* for the whole world. But if we only address systemic evil, we will leave people fed but spiritually dead. My friends, do not ever abandon justice, not until Christ returns and restores the whole world. But do not fail to declare the central gospel message: that Jesus died on the cross and rose again for our personal rebellion against God! We must address how the gospel treats the deepest problem—the problem of the sinful human heart. Anything less will always be hopelessly inadequate!"

WHY THE BAD NEWS OF SIN IS GOOD NEWS FOR PEOPLE

We have seen that the Bible describes sin as both unbelief and idolatry. In today's culture I have found that the concept of idolatry (turning to God-substitutes instead of God to give our life meaning) is often easier for people to grasp than the idea of having offended a righteous, holy God through unbelief. At the right time we will need to explain both aspects of sin, but I want to close this chapter by exploring how the issue of idolatry can be deeply relevant to unbelievers.

While we were living in the UK, I often went to the same London hair salon, and my hairdresser's name was Theo. As trust grew between us, Theo told me he was gay. He shared his life with me, and I shared my life and faith with him. While he respected my faith, he wasn't sure if God existed.

One day I arrived at the salon, and when I greeted Theo I realized that he was very low. As I sat in the chair, I put my hand on his arm and said, "Theo, are you going to tell me what's wrong?" He looked at me and said, "Becky, you are the only customer all day who's even noticed that I'm depressed."

He continued, "You know I've had a partner for several years. He is someone I have cherished and adored. He has deep problems, but I felt our love could fix anything. To be very honest, I worshiped him. But last week he moved out. I am absolutely devastated, and I don't know where to turn. But you are a Christian, so are you going to tell me that our relationship was doomed because I'm a homosexual?"

I took a deep breath, and said, "Oh Theo, I am so grieved to see you in this much pain. Actually, I think the issue you are struggling with is deeper than sexual identity. In fact, I have a straight friend, Anna, who just told me the exact same thing: she met the love of her life and was certain that their love would heal them both. But he recently left her for another woman, and she's now clinically depressed. Yet what I find interesting is that you both told me that you worshiped your partners, which is very insightful."

"Why is that insightful?" he asked.

"Because God has given us worshiping natures; we've been created to love and worship God. But where we run into trouble is when we try to worship something other than God—when we put something else in God's place. That can be good things or bad things, but God-substitutes will always fail us because they aren't big enough to ultimately build our lives upon."

Theo said, "That is exactly what my partner told me! He said I was trying to make him my everything and expecting him to meet my every need. He even said, 'I'm not god! It's way beyond my pay grade, and frankly it's exhausting.'"

I said, "Yes, it's why God-substitutes never work—because we are asking them to give us what only God can give: identity, purpose, and being totally understood and perfectly loved. The Bible even has a word for relying on God-substitutes—idolatry."

Theo looked at me in astonishment and said, "So you're telling me that, according to the Bible, my suffering is actually due to the fact that I've been worshiping the wrong thing?"

"Exactly! And Theo, you are not alone!" I said. "All of us, myself included, have used God-substitutes. All of us have turned from God and how he created us to be. It's the primary reason for all the brokenness around us and in us. The Christian author C.S. Lewis put it this way: when you look at cars, they appear to be functioning independently, but they are not! Cars are made to run on petrol. If we put anything else in the tank, they cannot function properly.

"Theo, it's exactly the same with us. We've been created for a relationship with God: to live with God at the center of our lives. But all of us have turned from God and have tried to run our lives as if we are in charge. We've all used God-substitutes to give our lives meaning and purpose. The reason the Christian message is called 'good news' is because God loves us and has been seeking us for far longer than we realize. But we also need to own the bad news—that we have chosen something else in place of God."

"What scares me is that what you're saying makes so much sense," Theo answered. "That to find the love I've been searching for all my life, I have to get my relationship with God sorted first. But I couldn't come to God, Becky—not after all the things I've done."

"Theo," I replied, "the only reason any of us can come to God is because God loves us. Jesus came from heaven and died on the cross for our sin because everyone needs God's forgiveness. There isn't anything we can do to deserve such a gift except to thank Jesus for all he has done for us, tell him we are sorry for our sin, and invite Jesus to come into our lives as Lord."

Theo said, "Becky, only the staff know this, but I've decided to go back to my home country to try to recover. This is my last week here. But I want to thank you for your friendship and for what you've just said. Thank you for speaking plainly without making me feel judged. Thank you for saying that you've also tried God-substitutes. Thank you for telling me that God loves me and wants a relationship with me when I am feeling so worthless. You've already given me some books and a Bible, so I think it's time that I start reading them."

When we said goodbye, it was poignant and heartfelt.

When people sense our compassion and love, and when they see that we ourselves identify as sinners and that we aren't looking down on them in judgment, it enables them to "hear" us, because they don't feel we are standing above them in judgment.

Why did I focus my conversation with Theo in the way that I did? Because Theo's deepest problem was that he did not understand where true human fulfillment comes from. While I believe that the Bible is clear about God's design for human sexuality (for more on this, see Abdu Murray's *Saving Truth* or Sam Allberry's *Is God Anti-gay?*), the root of Theo's problem was that he had made an idol of human love. If he had been in a straight relationship, the idol would have been the same. Theo and Anna were suffering deeply because they were both confused at the same point: that what makes us truly human and whole, and enables us to receive what our hearts have been searching for all along, is God.

Only God properly defines us. It is only through our relationship with God that we find our true identity and receive what we most need: forgiveness, reconciliation with God, identity, purpose, and the love that will never leave us. God is our Creator and therefore he is the only one big enough for us to build our lives upon. The tragedy of our sinfulness is that we lie to ourselves, raising up false gods that can never satisfy and ignoring the Creator who can. We deny ourselves the One who makes sense of life and satisfies our souls, because we're so determined to rule ourselves and make our own meaning and purpose.

The wonderful news of the gospel is that our sin and God's righteous judgment on sin do not have the last word. The very things we long for—to be understood and loved and received in our brokenness—have been made possible by the God who sent Jesus to rescue us, because "while we were still sinners, Christ died for us" (Romans 5 v 8).

So it's time to look at God's glorious solution, which changed all of history and eternity—the cross of Christ.

QUESTIONS FOR REFLECTION

- What are some ways you have learned in this chapter on how to talk about sin with unbelievers? What attitude do you need when discussing the fact that it's a problem that we all share?

- Which of the common objections discussed here do you come across most often? How would you answer these objections?

- We live in a culture that says the way to be happy is to think positive thoughts. But the story of Theo reveals that in order to experience the joy of the gospel, we need to face the mess. How can facing and understanding what our problem is actually be a help?

CHAPTER EIGHT

THE CROSS: GOD'S REMEDY

"The cross is the point where God and sinful man merge with a crash and the way to life is opened—but the crash is on the heart of God." (Oswald Chambers)

It is fascinating how in our post-Christian culture, when truth is no longer perceived in any objective or absolute sense, artists still seek to understand life's meaning (or lack thereof) through their art. One theme that appears frequently—in films, novels, sculptures, plays, and paintings—is the notion that the human race is disconnected.

The English author, atheist, and celebrated humanist E.M. Forster wrote in *Howard's End*, his 1910 novel that was made into a film, the famous, enigmatic epigraph, "Only connect." Forster believed that the heart of humanity's problem stemmed from deep disconnection: in our relationships with each other, in our relationship with ourselves, and in our relationship with nature. Forster believed that the only way for society to be healed was to learn how to humanly connect.

Stephen Spielberg, the acclaimed film producer, said in a television interview that nearly all of his films deal with the underlying theme of homesickness because people are discon-nected and pining for the place where they will feel safe and loved, like the extra-terrestrial in the film *ET*, who famously longed to go home.

This assessment is absolutely correct: the human race is dis-connected. However, as we've seen, the Bible explains that our "disconnect" is not merely a human-relations problem—it is in fact a God problem. God disconnected the human race from himself because of sin. That is why sin is actually best under-stood as a relational term, because, as the theologian Douglas John Hall puts it, "the foundational relationship of human life—our relation with God—is broken; and this brokenness shows up in all our other relations" (quote in Rutledge, *The Crucifixion*, page 127).

So why don't we just fix the problem? Because sin has caused us, as the Reformer Martin Luther said, to be "curved in" on our-selves (*Lectures on Romans*). We lack the power to fix the problem because we cannot extricate ourselves from the power of sin. No amount of religious or moral effort on our part can effect a sig-nificant change—nor, of course, can it make up for what we have already done. As the author Fleming Rutledge notes, the predica-ment of fallen humanity is "so serious, so grave, so irremediable from within, that nothing short of divine intervention can rectify it" (*The Crucifixion*, page 127).

That is why a self-help program cannot help us. Our need for forgiveness and a new start and a new nature can only be met by a power and love we do not possess. We need a radical love which forgives and forbears—we need a power outside ourselves to deliver and rescue us. Who has the power to take what is ter-ribly wrong and make it right?

The gospel proclaims that help has come. Sin and judgment are not the end of the story. Though God owed us nothing, in his mercy and grace he sent his divine Son from heaven on a rescue mission, in order to redeem a people for himself and to restore everything under Christ (Ephesians 1 v 10).

Christ came from heaven and solved the greatest crisis of our planet: our disconnection from God. That is why the death and resurrection of Jesus Christ lie at the very heart of the Christian faith and are the turning point of human history.

WHAT KIND OF GOD?

Why is the cross essential as our means of deliverance, wholeness and peace?

Because at the cross, the perfect and permanent sacrifice for our sin was made. Jesus died on the cross as "the lamb of God, who takes away the sin of the world" (John 1 v 29). When we repent and turn to Christ in faith, our sins are forgiven, our past is wiped clean, and we are given a brand new start because the penalty for our sin was paid by God himself! When the just judgment of the holy God had to fall, God the Son became our substitute, and the wrath of God the Father fell on him. It is a remarkable fact: we are proud sinners, but the final sacrifice for our sin and pride is God—a willing, loving substitute who stood in our place. The late John Stott noted,

> "For the essence of sin is man substituting himself for God, while the essence of salvation is God substituting himself for man. Man asserts himself against God and puts himself where only God deserves to be; God sacrifices himself for man and puts himself where only man

deserves to be. Man claims prerogatives that belong to God alone; God accepts penalties that belong to man alone." (*The Cross of Christ*, page 160)

We will never be able fully to comprehend the divine love that sent Jesus to the cross or fathom all that Jesus willingly endured on the cross. We get a hint in the Garden of Gethsemane when we see Jesus' profound sorrow as he contemplated what he was about to face on the cross (Matthew 26 v 36-46; Luke 22 v 39-46). But our deepest clue is in hearing Jesus' loud cry from the cross: "My God, my God, why have you forsaken me?" (Matthew 27 v 46). His cry, echoing Psalm 22 v 1, gives a glimpse into the divine cost of reconciling humanity to God: "God made him who had no sin to be sin for us, so that in him we might become the righteousness of God" (2 Corinthians 5 v 21). At the cross, Jesus took upon himself the sins of the world, bearing God's judgment of sin as the perfect and final sacrifice for all who believe in him (1 John 2 v 2, 23-25).

Just as sin separates us from God's loving presence, so Jesus was separated from that loving presence. That reality, far more than the nails and suffocation, is why the cross was so excruciating. To pay the price for human sin Jesus had to experience the utter anguish and abandonment of being forsaken by his Father and bearing his judgment for sin. That is what hell is—to be severed from the loving presence of God—and hell is what Jesus' agony was about, because through all eternity the Son of God had never known a moment apart from the love of his Father—and yet that is precisely what he knew on the cross.

All we can ask is "What kind of God willingly sacrifices so much so that he can be in relationship with his creation?" God the Father did not start loving us after Jesus went to the cross.

God's love for us—the love of both Father and Son—sent him there. The cross did not simply procure grace; it flowed from grace. Christ took our sinfulness into himself and overcame in himself what could not be overcome in human life. That is why the cross is the dividing line of human history. In every facet of God's action on the cross we see divine love at work.

More than any other act of history, the cross reveals why the good news of Jesus Christ is truly a gospel of grace.

But... if the cross offers people the possibility of a restored relationship with God and the promise of forgiveness, then why doesn't everyone see the cross as the best news ever?

THE CROSS: HOW THE WORLD SEES IT

How do we communicate the necessity of the cross in remedying sin when people believe they are innocent? We saw in the previous chapter that skeptics often grasp the idea of sin as idolatry. But the idea that all humanity has rebelled against a righteous and holy God, who is justified in his anger towards our sin, does not resonate with most non-Christians. It challenges the modern view that human nature is essentially good. And it makes people wonder why a loving God can't lighten up a bit. As a skeptic recently told me, "I am very forgiving of my flaws. Why can't God just be more tolerant, like I am with myself?"

Yet sudden cultural change often affects how people see reality, and it can open unexpected doors for us to talk about even the more difficult aspects of the gospel. Take the recent near-global phenomenon of women standing up in protest against sexual assault and harassment through the #MeToo movement.

The trigger that started this in the news cycle was the alleged crimes of one Hollywood film producer, who at the time of writing is being tried in court. A world-renowned actress voiced what many are now saying: "Don't tell me [this Hollywood producer] is an addict who needs rehab, or that he's psychologically wounded and needs therapy. He is a predator who needs prison!"

But why isn't this actress exhibiting the same tolerance that my skeptic friend insisted that God must have? Because when someone has been deeply sinned against, people feel moral outrage, and they want justice, not soft psychological explanations. And they are right. What they are acknowledging is that there are things that are deeply wrong, and wrong things deserve punishment—and that some wrongdoing cannot be tolerated, and that forgiveness cannot always be extended for free.

I Don't Really Need Forgiveness

I have a friend who is competent, successful, and assured of her own goodness. She said she never saw the need for a "crutch" like believing in God. Recently she told me of her outrage upon learning that her niece had been sexually assaulted by her boss. We talked at length and I listened with sympathy and concern. Towards the end of our conversation, I said, "Mary, we've had several conversations about faith. I want to be sure you know that the God of the Bible is morally outraged by what has happened to your niece. He stands against all forms of injustice and abuse."

Mary said, "Well, if there is a God, then he needs to do something about the horrible moral mess on our planet, and he clearly hasn't!"

"Mary, God has done something!" I responded. "It is why he sent his Son, Jesus, to die on the cross for our sin."

She said, "But Becky, what that predator did wasn't Jesus'

126

fault! Her boss is the one who needs to be punished—not Jesus. Otherwise, where's the justice?"

"You have hit the nail on the head," I replied. "You are right that crimes must have consequences; otherwise justice becomes a mockery. But what if the problem is larger and wider than we realize? Clearly, some people commit more outrageous and blatant sin than others, but in God's eyes we have all rebelled. All of us have chosen to run our own lives. It is why our planet is in this mess. You are also correct that it isn't God's fault that the human race rebelled. Yet the extraordinary message of the gospel is that God let the punishment for our sin fall on himself. God stepped in by sending Jesus. The righteous died for the unrighteous, so that we can be restored to God through our faith in Jesus."

She answered, "Becky, you know that I'm not a Christian. I have always laughed at the Christian belief that we're all sinners, but I'm not laughing anymore. I used to believe in my own goodness, but what I've come to see isn't just the evil of that predator—it's the murderous rage that I feel towards him. What this experience has taught me is that none of us are innocent."

It was the first crack I had ever seen in her view of herself. For the first time, she was wondering not just whether others might not be as good as she had assumed, but whether she might not be as good as she had supposed. We need to show people that their response of anger and indignation over horrific wrongdoing is something that God feels as well. It could be the catalyst that helps them understand why God's anger and judgment over human sin is justified. And if, like Mary, their response to evil goes from proper indignation to desiring murderous revenge— and they learn painful truth about themselves—it may also be what helps them see why they need outside help.

We point people to the cross so they can see why God's solution to evil is so radical, so undeserved, and so unprecedented. The truth is that all of us—from clergy to the kindly moral philosopher to those guilty of violent crimes—have sinned and can only be made right with God through the death of Christ.

I'm Too Bad to Receive Forgiveness

Of course, not everyone thinks they're a good person. Many realize, and are crushed by the realization, that they're entirely the opposite. Over the years I have heard so many people say something to the effect of "But even if Christianity is true, I could never come to God. He wouldn't want me—not after everything I have done." I also hear variations of this from sincere Christians who have trouble believing that God will forgive them for their past sins.

I met Katy at a conference where I was speaking, and Katy asked to talk with me afterwards. She told me that she and her fiancé were leaders of the youth ministry in their church when they discovered she was pregnant. They felt too ashamed to tell their pastor.

"So we did the only thing we felt was an option," she went on. "I had an abortion. Becky, that was ten years ago. I don't know where to go with my guilt, because what I keep thinking is, 'How could I have done it? How could I have been capable of taking the life of my innocent baby?'"

I prayed an urgent silent prayer, asking God to give me a word for this distraught woman. And he did. Summoning up my courage, I said, "Katy, I don't understand why you're so surprised. Because this isn't the first death of an innocent that you are responsible for—it's the second. The cross shows all of us as crucifiers—aborters or non-aborters, religious or atheists. All of us are responsible for the death of the only true innocent who ever lived.

"Jesus gave his life as a gift. He chose to die for our human rebellion. Do you think there is any human sin that did not nail Jesus to the cross? The German Reformer Martin Luther said, 'We carry Christ's nails in our pockets.' So, if you are responsible for the death of the only true innocent who ever lived, why are you so surprised that you and your fiancé are responsible for the death of a lesser innocent? I'm surprised that you're surprised."

For the first time she stopped crying. I held my breath.

"You're right," she said. "Jesus went to the cross for all of our sin, but I've just realized something. I have felt more guilt over the death of my own son than the death of God's Son. But if the cross shows me that I've done the worst thing imaginable—that I am responsible for the death of Jesus—and that has been forgiven, then how can any other sin not be forgiven?"

With tears streaming down her face, she said, "Oh, Becky, this is truly amazing grace!"

That day I saw a woman transformed by her new understanding of the meaning of the cross. The paradox of the cross is that it insists on highlighting our evil, in order to leave us with absolutely no doubt that whatever we have done, we can be forgiven. If God is willing to forgive us for the death of Christ, then is there any other sin we confess that could be more grievous than that? That is why we run to the cross, and call others to come with us—in freedom, even joy, because though we are undeserving, God's solution is so wonderful!

Katy was already a Christian, but I meet many unbelievers who also experience shame and guilt. The wonderful message of the gospel is that we do not need to excuse or ignore sin, or be crushed by it, or try to work it off! We can give our sin to Jesus because he dealt with sin, finally and absolutely, at the cross.

At the cross, we see the worst of ourselves, and it would be unbearable if we did not in the same second see God's loving forgiveness. Through faith in Christ we can let go of our shame and guilt, and start walking in freedom and joy because, through Jesus' death and resurrection, we can be forgiven and made new.

WHY THE CROSS IS SUCH GOOD NEWS

How do we help people to see why the cross has such relevance for their lives, particularly if they do not believe they are sinners? We began this chapter by looking at how even secular artists recognize that we are disconnected and homesick for something we cannot quite articulate. How can we help skeptics who are not in a moment of crisis (like my friend whose niece had been assaulted) or consciously burdened by their sin (like Katy) to see how the cross satisfies their human longings?

Identity and Security for the Lost and Insecure

Western cultural conversation is dominated by the subject of identity: understanding who we are and where we fit. Psychologists tell us that the issue of identity produces more anxiety, confusion, and insecurity in our day than it has in any other time in history. Sociologists note that the way we view identity has changed. In earlier times, identity was something that was ascribed: our parents and our social place in society determined our identity and work. There was greater security but also less freedom. In the 21st century, our identity is achieved: we are told we can create our own identities and destinies. As the pop star Lady Gaga once said in an interview, "I live to recreate myself!" While today we have more freedom than our ancestors, we have less security—and we also have greater anxiety, anger, and therapy bills!

Sociologists have also pointed out that people today seek identity through external means such as our how we look to others: the cars we drive, the clothes we wear, or the friends we associate with. But it has proven to be a horribly inadequate basis for providing a secure sense of identity. It has led to a shallow and consumer-driven approach to identity that leaves us feeling vulnerable and uncertain.

More recently, many people have tended to seek identity through group identity—particularly if we are part of a group that sees itself (often with justification) as oppressed and victims of injustice. But again, this leads to insecurity, because there is a constant pressure to prove you belong, and to sign up to your group's current thinking in every way, for fear of being told you no longer have a place. Ironically, in an age of expressive individualism, you are only loved while you conform to the norms and expectations—and demands—of the group. And it is reductive and unsatisfying, because it defines us as a particular intersection of various labels or identities, when in truth we are each more than the sum of our gender, sexuality, race, and so on.

The good news of the gospel is that the Creator God alone knows the person we truly are:

> My frame was not hidden from you, when I was made in secret ... Your eyes have seen my unformed substance and in your book were all written the days that were ordained for me, when as yet there was not one of them.
>
> (Psalm 139 v 15-16, NASB)

How does the cross answer our identity and insecurity issues? It reveals that we do not have to pretend or spend energy on projecting a false, invented persona, because God knows who we truly are. God knows what it is to be a victim of injustice, for he experienced the worst injustice ever perpetrated on a human, by humans. And God knows us at our very worst, and he loves us anyway: "While we were still sinners, Christ died for us" (Romans 5 v 8).

That means we don't have to prove our worth because in Christ we can be forgiven, and through Christ we are accepted and adopted—our most central identity becomes that we are a child of God. We walk with confidence and freedom because we know the One who runs the world is a perfect, kind Father who calls us his sons and daughters. The cross proves that God's love and acceptance of us isn't based on our performance but on Jesus' performance. It is in Christ that we find our deepest security. The wonderful message of the gospel is that what we have been looking for and longing for is what Jesus offers.

Comfort for the Suffering

A Franciscan University in Ohio recently posted a series of ads on Facebook to promote some of its online theology programs. But Facebook rejected one of them because it included a representation of the crucifixion. The monitors at Facebook said the reason for their rejection was that they found the depiction of the cross "shocking, sensational, and excessively violent."

The Franciscan University of Steubenville responded with a blog post that no doubt surprised Facebook: they agreed with Facebook's assessment! The Franciscan university posted:

> "Indeed the crucifixion of Christ was all of those things.
> It was the most sensational action in history: man

executed his God. It was shocking, yes: God deigned to take on flesh and was 'obedient unto death, even death on a cross' (Philippians 2 v 8). And it was certainly excessively violent: a man scourged to within an inch of his life, nailed naked to a cross and left to die, all the hate of all the sin in the world poured out its wrath upon his humanity."

They went on to say that it wasn't the nails that kept Jesus on the cross but his love for mankind:

"He was God, he could have descended from the cross at any moment. No, it was love that kept him there. Love for you and for me, that we might not be eternally condemned for our sins but might have life eternal with him and his Father in heaven."
(https://blogs.franciscan.edu/faculty/he-was-rejected/
accessed 11/4/19)

Sometimes skeptics ask me, "Why was the cross so shockingly violent and brutal?" Here we have to return to the Bible's unblinking, unrelenting portrayal of sin and evil on earth. The whole of Scripture testifies that sin isn't merely the problem of an evil few—everyone shares the problem of sin. Given the right circumstances and pressures, all of us are capable of almost anything.

Yet people tend to give themselves a pass for personal sin with the weak excuse of "Hey, no one is perfect." This is when we need to point out other aspects of sin—the monstrous evil that is beyond human comprehension or rational explanation: world wars; the horror of African slavery; wholesale genocides like the Holocaust or Cambodia or Rwanda or ISIS's treatment of the Yazidi people in Iraq. That may help people see why the gruesomeness of the remedy needs to match the gruesomeness of the crime. As the academic and writer Stephen Westerholm notes, "Only such a catastrophic remedy as the cross could match our catastrophic predicament" (*Apocalyptic Paul,* ed. Beverly Roberts Gaventa, page 200).

In fact, it is the awfulness of the cross that gives comfort to those who have suffered awful things in this world. In my experience, people who have deeply suffered, especially over a period of time, are usually not asking for explanations anymore. They want our presence, our tears, and our love as we sit with them in their suffering. Yet, we can offer more than that.

I had the privilege of living in Jerusalem for three years in the 1980s. Without question, the most powerful experience of my time there was hearing so many stories from Holocaust survivors. Again and again I asked myself, "How does faith in a personal, loving God survive these stories?" After hearing a particularly unbearable story, I went out on the balcony of our apartment, which overlooked Jerusalem, and I prayed and wept. As I stood up to go inside, I looked again at the view and saw in the far distance the olives trees surrounding the Garden of Gethsemane. I had seen it many times before—but never with such impact.

Why? Because I realized at that moment that the only thing that enables us to bear horrific, unjust suffering is the cross of Christ— the scars of which he bears even in heaven! The sinless One died for the sinful. To our human perspective this was the greatest injustice anyone could ever experience. And Jesus went through it for one reason: because of the love of God for his creatures.

It is an amazing thought that in all of the religions of the world, it is only the Christian God who bears scars. With all the suffering in our world, it would be hard to trust a God who had not suffered. But Jesus has suffered, and he didn't have to; he chose to! His scars reveal that he understands the difficulties of life far better than we do. He's been here. He knows. "For we do not have a high priest who is unable to empathize with our weaknesses, but we have one who has been tempted in every way, just as we are—yet he did not sin" (Hebrews 4 v 15).

We saw in the early chapters of Genesis that we are wonderfully created. After humanity rebelled against God, we also saw the horrific impact that sin had on our planet and our desperate need for rescuing and deliverance. But the message of the cross is that we can be wonderfully restored. It is the heart of our faith and must always be the heart of our message. Jesus died for our sins. And he is alive forever more—which is where we turn next.

QUESTIONS FOR REFLECTION

- Who do you know who thinks they are too good to need forgiveness? Who do you know who thinks they are too bad to be offered forgiveness? How will these two views shape the ways you communicate the message of the cross to each?
- Which of the common objections discussed here do you come across most often? How would you answer these objections?
- How can knowing that the scars of Jesus "reveal that he understands the difficulties of life far better than we do" comfort people in trials and suffering? How can this aspect of the cross help you in communicating the goodness of God to those who are hurting?

CHAPTER NINE

THE RESURRECTION: EVERYTHING HAS CHANGED

"Jesus' resurrection is the beginning of God's new project not to snatch people away from earth but to colonize earth with the life of heaven." (N.T. Wright)

The renowned child psychiatrist Robert Coles told this story in a graduate class I attended at Harvard University many years ago: "A highly regarded psychiatrist recently told me in despair: 'I have been doing therapy with a man for 15 years. He is as angry, as self-centered, and as mean as he was the first day he walked into my office. The only difference is that now he knows *why* he is so angry and mean.'"

Dr. Coles pointed out that although the psychiatrist provided his client with insight as to how his childhood emotional wounding had affected his adult dysfunction, the man still hadn't changed. Coles asked, "Could we conclude that what this man needed wasn't just information but transformation? But is transformation possible for human beings?"

The message of the resurrection is that transformation is possible! Because, while Christianity is deeply realistic about the human condition, it is profoundly optimistic that human beings can be changed. For if the cross enables us to see our problem and how God has solved it, then the resurrection provides objective data that human transformation is possible.

Why is this? Because even when a massive stone was placed and sealed over the entrance of Jesus' tomb and soldiers were posted to guard the tomb for three days, nevertheless the impossible happened. Jesus rose from the dead! When the worst that our world could muster—execution—was brought down on Jesus, God blasted the tomb open and brushed death aside, and the entire universe would never be the same. The Roman government and the Jewish leaders turned Jerusalem upside down trying to find the body of Jesus. It was all they needed to prove that Jesus and his claims were a hoax. Yet his corpse was never discovered.

If the Spirit of God could raise Jesus from death to life—if he could revitalize dead brain cells, restore collapsed lungs, restart a heart, and give Jesus his transformed, glorified new body—then that same Spirit can cause those who are spiritually dead to become alive to God! The Spirit stirs spiritual understanding and new life in uncomprehending hearts (1 Corinthians 2 v 11-15; John 3 v 3-8). And that is not the end of his work but the beginning, for he goes on changing us: the "power working in us is the same as the mighty strength which God used when he raised Christ from death" (Ephesians 1 v 19-20). Everyone who puts their trust in Christ receives the transforming, resurrecting power of the Holy Spirit.

A CORPSE WALKED OUT OF A TOMB

The Bible tells us that over a forty-day period the risen Jesus appeared, physically, to a multitude of people. The Gospel of Luke says that on the Sunday after Jesus died, the disciples had locked themselves in a room because of fear and confusion. Imagine the shock, shame, and fear that engulfed the disciples. Their leader was gone, they were confused and uncertain of the future, and they didn't know what step to take next. Jesus had died by crucifixion: that indescribably horrific method of death that the Romans reserved for the most heinous criminals and enemies of the state. Even worse, the Jewish leaders and religious authorities—those who of all people should have recognized who he was—had approved of his death.

It is important to realize that, at this point, the disciples would not have seen Jesus' death as a glorious conquest to be celebrated but as an intolerable defeat and catastrophic failure. They had banked everything on Jesus, but now their hopes had been snuffed out. They were so hopeless that not one of them said, on that first Easter Sunday, "Hold on a minute—it's the third day since he died, and several times he said he'd be killed but that he'd rise on the third day. I wonder if he'll appear?" No one seems to have even considered the possibility.

Then suddenly, Luke tells us, "Jesus himself stood among them and said 'Peace be with you.'" (Luke 24 v 36). Walls of thick stone and a barricaded door could not keep Jesus out. What was the disciple's response? "They were startled and frightened, thinking they saw a ghost" (v 37)! How did Jesus convince them that it was truly him? In surprisingly ordinary ways.

Jesus appealed to their physical senses: "Why are you troubled … ? Look at my hands and feet. It is I myself! Touch me and see; a ghost does not have flesh and bones, as you see I have" (v 38-39). Then he showed them his hands and sides so they could see his wounds. Next he ate a piece of broiled fish. They were still incredulous, skeptical, and terrified.

Their final stage of doubt, Luke says, was that "they still did not believe it because of joy and amazement" (v 41). If this was really Jesus, then it meant that all of Jesus' claims were true. God was actually vindicating Jesus right before their eyes! Imagine the awe that pervaded that room as they began to realize what they were seeing: Jesus is alive!

What changed the apostles from being frightened and disillusioned to being ready to die for their faith? First, the apostles saw with their own eyes that the tomb was empty. Jesus was alive, and they had talked with him face to face! Second, they saw Jesus' wounds, which must have helped them understand that Christ was the literal fulfillment of Isaiah 53: the one who had been "pierced for our transgressions," and the one "by [whose] wounds we are healed" (v 5). His wounds represented his mission's glorious success; they were the proof that God had accepted Jesus' sacrifice for our sin on the cross.

Third, the risen Jesus showed the disciples how the Scriptures (the Old Testament) pointed to him and predicted that the Messiah would suffer, die, and be raised from the dead (v 45-46). This was a critical fact in strengthening their faith, since death by crucifixion was so hideous and shameful in their culture.

The ascension of Christ from earth to heaven was the final act in the drama of redemption. His mission completed, Jesus Christ was exalted to his former glory "far above all rule and authority and power and domination … not only in this age but also in that which is to come" (Ephesians 1 v 21).

The risen Jesus then sent the promised gift of the Holy Spirit, so that his followers would be filled with the power and presence of his Spirit (Acts 2). It's no wonder that Christianity exploded across the known world in the first century. God was using fully convinced Spirit-filled followers of Jesus to turn the world upside down!

Everything changed, and that change began on that first Easter Sunday morning when a corpse walked out of a tomb. "If Christ had not been raised, our preaching is useless and so is your faith" (1 Corinthians 15 v 14). But he *was* raised!

THE RESURRECTION: HOW THE WORLD SEES IT

There are two things to keep in mind when talking about the resurrection with our skeptic friends. They will need to hear both the rational (objective) evidence and the experiential (subjective) evidence. We need to be prepared to offer both. Let's look at the rational approach first and then at the experiential evidence.

Here are the most common rational objections to the claim of the resurrection, or, to put it another way, the strongest alternative explanations to the Bible's claim that Jesus rose.

People in Jesus' Day were Naïve and Gullible

Skeptics argue that people today are far too sophisticated and skeptical to believe in the claims of miracles, such as Jesus being raised to life from the grave. People living in Jesus' day were simply more gullible and naïve than we are today. C.S. Lewis called this "chronological snobbery": when people from a later generation assume that they are more educated and not so easily duped as those of earlier generations. Yet consider the disciple we call "doubting Thomas"—he flat-out refused to believe the other disciples when they insisted that they'd seen Christ and that he was alive. Thomas retorted, "Unless I see the nail marks in his hands and put my finger where the nails were, and put my hand into his side, I will not believe" (John 20 v 25). It wasn't until the risen Jesus appeared to Thomas and said, "Reach out your hand and put it into my side. Stop doubting and believe" that Thomas believed and worshiped him (v 27-28). Clearly there were at least some people living in Jesus' day who were no less skeptical than we are today—perhaps even more so! First-century people knew just as well as we do that the laws of nature dictate that dead people stay dead, and there was nothing in Jewish theology to anticipate a specific, individual resurrection before the final, universal resurrection for judgment that Jewish theology taught. So for the disciples, neither their life experience nor their religious upbringings made them susceptible to being too easily convinced that Jesus had come back from the dead.

The Disciples Fantasized They'd Seen Him Alive

Some argue that because the disciples were expecting and longing to see Jesus alive, they simply fantasized that it had happened. But his followers clearly hadn't understood what Jesus meant when he said he would rise again, or they wouldn't have been so astonished and skeptical when they saw him. When he appeared to the disciples in that locked room, it took much convincing from Jesus to persuade them that it was really him. N.T. Wright convincingly argues in his book *The Resurrection of the Son of God* that the disciples never expected or even imagined that Jesus would be raised from the dead with a new body fit for heaven for the simple reason that no one in human history had ever seen such a thing happen. Lazarus was resuscitated but he didn't have the powers of a new resurrection body like Jesus did, and he would die again. Jews at that time believed in the resurrection of the dead at the end of history, but not the bodily resurrection of a single individual before the Messiah returned at the end of the age.

Wright also argues that it's difficult to come up with any historically plausible alternative explanations for the birth of the Christian movement. For example, Jews did not believe any human being was divine and should be worshiped—in fact, it was considered extreme blasphemy. What we need to ask skeptics then is "What changed the worldview of Jesus' followers seemingly overnight? What caused them to go from utter despair to having profound confidence, courage and joy? Why did Christianity grow so rapidly and with such power?" The Bible records that Jesus was seen by over 500 people at one time (1 Corinthians 15 v 6). How do we explain why decades later these same people not only publicly testified that they had seen the risen Lord but were willing to die rather than deny what they knew to be true?

The Bible Is Not Historically Reliable

This is an issue that has been long been debated, particularly recently. It is important to know the basic criteria that scholars and historians have devised to determine the historical authenticity of an ancient text. How early was the manuscript written? Was it written by eyewitnesses? Were there ancient documents written by non-Christians that verify the basic facts of Jesus' life? Was there any contradictory literature written around Jesus' time that refutes the claims of his followers? Space prevents me from going into more detail: two great, and fairly short, recent books on the subject are *Is Jesus History?* by John Dickson and *Can We Trust the Gospels?* by Peter Williams.

"I ask, 'How can you intelligently reject something you've never explored?'"

I also find it helpful in discussions like these to ask, "Do you agree that the New Testament must meet the basic historical criteria that validate whether a piece of ancient literature is historically reliable?" I have never met anyone who does not agree. I also ask, "Do you also agree that we cannot ask more, or less, simply because the ancient document in question is the Bible?" Again nearly everyone will answer yes. And then, if someone seems open to considering faith, I ask, "If the Bible turned out to be historically reliable, would you be willing to investigate the life of Jesus in the Gospels with me? Otherwise, how can you intelligently reject something you've never explored?"

Miracles Are Impossible, so Jesus Did Not Rise

A miracle is an event that cannot be explained through the laws of nature—but what determines whether we think miracles are possible depends on our assumptions.

An atheist believes that all things in the universe are subject to natural physical laws, so it follows that they'll think miracles are impossible because miracles represent a suspension of the natural order. If someone believes in a God who created the universe, then it follows that they'll think that miracles are possible, and even that they are to be expected!

Skeptics cannot prove, in any absolute sense, that God does not exist because they cannot prove what the first cause of creation was, or how life came to be. They cannot actually rule out miracles, rationally. Of course, skeptics can answer by saying that Christians cannot prove the existence of God either, because we cannot make the invisible God become visible. This is a great starting point for discussion because the biblical claim is that God did become visible through Jesus Christ! That is why it is so important to invite skeptics to consider the possibility that God exists by taking a look at the person of Jesus and seeing what they make of this man who said he was God and who backed up his claims with his actions.

The point is that while believers and skeptics both base their positions on what they believe to be credible evidence, both sides are ultimately operating from a position of faith. While we must listen respectfully and seek to understand another point of view, it is important to make clear that our faith is not based on irrationality or superstitions but on credible evidence that needs to be considered.

We need to tell people that Christ is risen! But we need to do so not argumentatively, but lovingly. When it comes to the resurrection, too many of us win the argument and lose the person. As Ravi Zacharias says, we need to answer well, but to…

> "… do it with humility, because ultimately the answer is in a person, the person of Christ, not in an argument … Know how to present the answer, but do it with gentleness and meekness."
> (https://apologetics315.com/2013/02/ravi-zacharias-interview-transcript/, accessed 12/23/19)

You cannot debate someone into the kingdom of God, but you can debate them away from looking at its King. We must be bold in our proclamation that Jesus is risen, and that this proves the validity of his claims and of what he says about sin and salvation—but we need to do it lovingly. We need to show in how we treat people that, for us, the resurrection is not simply a historical event but a present reality.

So there is another kind of "evidence" that is needed as well. The issue isn't only whether the resurrection happened but whether it matters. What difference does it actually make in our lives today?

How Do You Know God Is Real?

There are many ways in which the resurrection addresses our needs. I have been struck by how often seekers and skeptics tell me that they feel powerless: whether it's dealing with a rebellious teenager, getting out of debt, breaking a destructive habit, changing or leaving a corrosive relationship, or having an impossible boss; the list is endless. They recognize they need help, but they aren't sure where to turn. What I tell them is that we need a power much greater than our own to help us with the trials of life. It isn't that Christians don't have problems. We do! But when we become followers of the risen Jesus, he gives us the Holy Spirit, who empowers and helps us in the ups and downs of life.

Mary was a friend who had recently become engaged to Tom. One day she told me that Tom had received money from an inheritance when he was just a teenager. A close relative had put the money in a bank account for when Tom came of age, and now Tom needed the money to make a down payment for their first home. For six months Tom sent letters, texts, and emails, and left voicemails, asking for the money. But he received no response. Mary said, "Becky, we hate doing this, but we don't see any other option. We are hiring a lawyer next week."

I said, "May I ask you a favor? Would you give my husband and me a week to pray and ask God for an answer, before you phone a lawyer?" She agreed, and I told her I'd call her in a week.

Four days later she phoned me and said, "Have you been praying for us like you said?" I assured her that we had been praying every day. Then she said, "You aren't going to believe this, but guess what arrived in our mail box today? A registered letter with a certified check for the whole amount! We couldn't believe it! Tom and I want to come and thank you and Dick in person!"

They came, and we had a thoroughly delightful evening. Tom strongly encouraged us to use our prayers to win the lottery! We explained that it wasn't our power that had done anything—it was God's power that had accomplished this. As Christians we were just doing what the Bible tells us to—we had poured out our hearts to God in prayer, asking him to help them.

"But why would God answer your prayers for us? We don't even go to church," Tom said.

Dick answered, "Because God wants you to know that he is real, and that he loves you and desires to have a relationship with you."

I haven't always seen prayers answered as dramatically as this prayer. Nor have I seen answered prayer always be the catalyst for conversion, though it was in this case. But when unbelievers see prayers answered, they want to hear more about who God is. Answered prayer reveals that the power doesn't reside in us but in God. It provides evidence that Christ truly rose from the dead and that he is alive. It shows skeptics that God has the love and the power that they so desperately need for life's trials.

WHY THE RESURRECTION IS SUCH GOOD NEWS

The resurrection speaks to perhaps our greatest felt need—the need to be known and loved.

After all, God has wired us to love and to be loved, to know and to be known. When Dick and I lived in Europe we did a lot of evangelistic ministry with university students. Often students shared with us their immense loneliness. One student said, "I have 300 'friends' online but no one I could turn to if I was in trouble—no one who really knows me and loves me. I need to know that someone has my back and will be there when I need them."

How is the resurrection of Jesus relevant to people like this? Because the risen Jesus assured the disciples that he would never leave them nor forsake them, and that he would send his Spirit to accompany them, and that Jesus would answer their prayers from heaven. The reason they could count on him was because he was alive from the dead!

The resurrection shows us that we are more than emotional and physical beings; we are also spiritual beings, who need God. It is our relationship with the risen Jesus that meets our longing for love, who is our true and reliable anchor in our uncertain world, and who gives our lives meaning and purpose. It's also why our love for unbelievers is so important—it provides the evidence that Jesus is alive.

In an earlier chapter I told the story of my London hairdresser, Theo, who returned to his country for rest and a sabbatical.

The next time I went to the hair salon, I had a new hairdresser, Ruth. She told me that right before Theo left, he shared at their staff meeting our entire conversation. I was stunned to hear Ruth repeat verbatim everything I had said. Ruth said, "The staff were so touched, Becky, by how you saw Theo's pain and reached out to him. We've been so worried about him. Theo said he always felt very loved by you, but that you also challenged him and made him think. Like when you told him that to find the love he was looking for, he needed to get his spiritual identity sorted first. That we get into trouble when we worship a person instead of God because no person can bear the weight of being our god. That really struck us, because most of us are struggling in our romantic relationships."

As I was about to leave, she added, "I hope you don't mind me asking, but we all wonder what you're like in your professional role as a Christian, when you speak to groups. One guy said, 'I wonder when she speaks to crowds if she still sounds like our Becky?'"

I said, "Ruth, it's amazing you are saying this, because the BBC has asked me to give a live talk for their Radio 4 program called *Sunday Morning Worship*. It's in three weeks, though I can't imagine the staff would be willing to get up at 8:30 in the morning!"

Sunday Morning Worship has been on Radio 4 for decades, and it still attracts almost 1½ million listeners (including the queen!)—and a surprising percentage of the listening audience aren't Christians. That morning, I spoke on the resurrection and geared my talk to skeptics. A week later I walked into the hair salon, and, to my astonishment, all the staff started clapping and said in unison, "We all got up and heard you!"

One young employee, Michael, said, "Becky, I was really looking forward to hearing you, but I had a rather boozy night on Saturday. I live with my parents, and when I came downstairs Sunday morning, my mum was sipping coffee at the kitchen table and listening to the radio. As I poured my coffee, I suddenly shouted, 'Oh my gosh, that's Becky on the radio! Turn it up!' Mum looked at me in amazement and said, 'You actually know the preacher?' I said, 'Yes, she's a friend of mine!'

"So as we sipped our coffees we listened to your talk. Mum and I spoke for a long time afterwards about what it would mean for us if Jesus had truly been resurrected. Mum thinks you may be right, and I said that even I might agree. But Becky, I'm still a young man. If I became a Christian, how much would it have to impact my current lifestyle?"

When I sat down in the chair, Ruth said, "Last Saturday I told my partner of five years that we had to get up early Sunday morning to hear you. As I've told you before, I vaguely believe in some kind of deity. My partner is an agnostic, and we have never had a discussion about faith. But after the radio show he said, 'You know, I am really intrigued by what Becky said. Do you think you could find any more videos of her online?'"

Ruth found a video, and they watched it on her iPad as they ate breakfast. When they went into the living room for coffee he said, "Why don't you try to find another one of her talks?" Unbelievably, they listened to a third talk!

To my great amusement, Ruth finished by saying, "Becky, that's the longest I've ever been in church in my entire life, and it was an absolute first for my partner! It's led to our having many conversations about faith. We aren't ready to visit a church yet, but can you suggest something to help us investigate further?"

As I was leaving, I asked Ruth what had caused the staff to get up so early to listen to a sermon.

"Because we saw how much you truly cared for Theo," she answered. "He had another client who is a Christian, but she was judgmental. And other clients would just tell him not to worry. But you saw his pain and even suggested that he had a deeper problem that he was overlooking. You helped him, and it really touched us."

People are watching us more than we realize, to see if our lives match our words. When they see the love of Christ demonstrated, it softens the soil and makes them curious to find out more about God. They are experiencing the transformation that the risen Jesus has caused in us even as they are hearing about the claims that the resurrection makes on them.

HOPE BEYOND THE GRAVE

We are living in a time of great turmoil and confusion, when many people feel vulnerable and frightened, even despairing, without knowing why. People need hope, and the resurrection of

Jesus gives them reason to hope, because the risen Christ promises to walk with his followers through life's difficulties and joys, and to greet us when we pass from this life to the next.

The purpose of the resurrection is not for us to sit back and wait for heaven, but to live in such a way that everything we are, say, and do (both the visual and verbal) causes unbelievers to want to investigate the life of Jesus; and then, when the time seems right, we can invite them to give their lives to Jesus so they too can experience his transforming, resurrection life as they walk with us towards eternity. As the late Eugene Peterson poignantly wrote, "The Bible is not a script for a funeral service, but it is the record of God always bringing life where we expected to find death. Everywhere it is a story of resurrection."

Yet the resurrection is not the end of the story. Because one day Christ will come again to earth at the end of human history—and in one sense, that is when life truly begins!

QUESTIONS FOR REFLECTION

- Why does the resurrection of Jesus offer profound hope for those who put their trust in him? How would you explain that hope to someone?
- Which of the common objections discussed here do you come across most often? How would you answer them?
- "Would you be willing to investigate the life of Jesus in the Gospels with me? Otherwise, how can you intelligently reject something you've never explored?" Is there someone you could invite to read a Gospel with you? Will you start praying about this and consider when you will ask them?

CHAPTER TEN

THE RETURN: MORE TO COME

"Joy, which was the small publicity of the pagan, is the gigantic secret of the Christian." (G.K. Chesterton)

The late Professor David Flusser, an orthodox Jewish scholar and respected authority on first-century Christianity and Judaism, was once asked, "As an orthodox Jew, you believe Messiah is coming. But if Messiah should come in your lifetime, what question would you ask him?"

"Oh, that's easy," Professor Flusser replied. "I would ask Messiah, 'Is this your first visit or your second?'"

The glory of all that Christ accomplished through his death and resurrection isn't the end of the gospel story. The Bible shouts from the rooftop that Jesus came to reconcile the world to God—and that he will come again! So Messiah is coming—and when Jesus comes from heaven to earth in his glorified resurrection body, it will be his second visit.

Why is the second coming of Christ so significant? Because when Christ returns, he will end human history as we know it. When Jesus first came to earth, he ushered in the kingdom of heaven, but he didn't erase all the effects of sin on our planet. Human beings would still experience hardship, injustice, disease, and death. It is only when Christ returns and brings the presence of heaven with him that all forms of evil—sin, Satan, and death—will be removed forever from earth. Christ will usher in a new and endless age: the age of the new heaven and the new earth, in which all things, including the community of God's redeemed people, will be made new: or perhaps more accurately, will be renewed.

The New Testament writers mention Christ's return over 300 times; about one out of every thirteen verses is about the second coming. The New Testament is practically bursting at the seams with this sense of expectation! We need to recapture the sense of lively expectation that was so prevalent in New Testament believers and live, as Paul says, in eager expectation of "the blessed hope—the glorious appearing of our great God and Savior, Jesus Christ" (Titus 2 v 13).

In this chapter we will look at three central aspects of Christ's return: the resurrection of the dead, the reckoning of his judgment, and the renewal of the earth. Then, as we've been doing in each chapter in this section, we will explore how each of these significant events has relevance to those who have been looking for their true home, and how to show that Christ's return is the good news that we have been longing for all along.

THE RESURRECTION OF THE DEAD

The Bible tells us that at Christ's return every eye shall see him (Revelation 1 v 7)! His appearing won't only be to those living at that time, or only to those who believe in him. Christ will command the dead from every generation to be raised to life. The whole world—every person who has ever lived—will see Christ in his glorified humanity, and God's indisputable truth will be revealed to the entire cosmos.

As Paul writes, "There shall certainly be a resurrection of both the righteous and the wicked" (Acts 2 v 15). Paul also says:

> Behold! I tell you a mystery. We shall not all sleep, but we shall all be changed, in a moment, in the twinkling of an eye, at the last trumpet. For the trumpet will sound, and the dead will be raised imperishable, and we shall be changed. (1 Corinthians 15 v 51-52)

The Bible tells us that Jesus' followers will receive new eternal bodies when Jesus returns. What will our new bodies be like? Like his (1 Corinthians 15 v 20)! When the risen Christ appeared, he wasn't a phantom or ghost. He ate real earthly food; he walked and talked at length with his disciples; and he could touch and be touched. But his body had extra-dimensional qualities that it didn't have before: he could pass through solid walls and suddenly appear out of nowhere.

At Christ's return the resurrection bodies we receive will be our own physical bodies, yet perfected and glorified (1 John 3 v 2). We will never age or be subject to decay, frailty, or death. It will be glorious.

NEW BODIES: HOPE IN SUFFERING

But how could receiving new bodies at the end of time possibly be relevant to unbelievers today? Because, sooner or later, all of us—believers and unbelievers—will experience trials. Even if we are spared serious suffering, there will most likely be someone we love who will experience great difficulty.

What makes suffering especially difficult for people today is that so many believe that the purpose of life is to feel good—and clearly suffering never makes anyone feel good. If this life is all there is, then physical pain or unfulfilled dreams are a disaster.

Yet, through the centuries, Christians have not regarded suffering as disastrous, nor something that precludes living with joy. Why? The apostle John wrote a letter to first-century churches, many of whom were facing severe persecution under the Emperor Nero. We call John's letter the book of Revelation. John gave his first readers courage in the midst of their suffering by writing about the second coming. He told them about the visions that God had allowed him to see of the new, eternal world to come. He reminded them that this life wasn't the only one. He also reminded them that they had a physical eternal life to look forward to. He said that their present suffering couldn't compare to the glory they would one day experience. By reminding them of the future glory that was to come, Revelation gave them hope and perseverance through their immense trials. The reality of Christ's return gives hope in suffering—and since everyone suffers, everyone needs that kind of hope.

How we handle suffering as Christians is an important part of our witness. I vividly remember taking my then young son David to hear Dave Dravecky speak. Dravecky, once an all-star professional baseball pitcher, was tragically diagnosed with cancer in his throwing arm. After countless cancer treatments, the surgeons finally had to amputate. In a lecture I heard him give and from which I kept my notes, he gave a tremendously moving testimony about coming to faith in Christ during his cancer battle:

> "In my early years my pitching arm was my entire identity: it made me famous, gave me status, gave me

confidence and security, and earned me lots of money. What I learned through my trauma was that the most important questions to ask were these: Is my sense of identity and purpose based on what is true? Is it big enough to build my life upon?"

As he said this, he slowly took off his jacket, and the visual image was unforgettable: the man standing before us not only had no right arm; he had no right shoulder. He asked:

"So tell me, was my pitching arm big enough to build my life upon?"

He then made two powerful points. First, we must build our lives upon what is true and eternal: faith in God through Jesus Christ. Second, this life isn't the only life:

"Now that I've finally put God first in my life, I still deeply love baseball but I can't throw a ball to my son, much less play the game," he said. "But I know that when Christ returns, he will give me a new body. On that day I will be able to throw a ball to God's glory and my sheer delight."

Why can Christians have hope in suffering? Because, just as Jesus triumphed over death and received a new transformed body, we will experience the very same when Christ returns at the end of history. Here is the greatest hope for those who are suffering from chronic pain, disease, illness, disability, or mental-health problems: if they place their faith in Christ, then they can look forward to an eternity free of struggle and experiencing freedom and wholeness. The future resurrection of the body isn't often used evangelistically—but it should be.

THE RECKONING

The Bible is clear that at the end of history the dead from every generation will be raised to life and Christ will judge all who have ever lived (John 5 v 28-29; 3 v 18, 36). There will be ultimate justice at last because God will rectify all wrongs and establish his righteous rule forever.

While this is welcoming (though sobering) news for believers, for unbelievers the idea of judgment seems implausible and unfair, particularly if they don't believe in sin in the first place. Yet, ironically, the same people who reject the idea of final divine judgment still long for justice. They know that something is desperately wrong with the world and must be made right. An agnostic said to me recently, "We are living on a planet where atrocities and evil are common occurrences. I simply can't make sense of a world where there is no cosmic justice."

Because his primary complaint was the lack of cosmic justice, I spoke to him about Christ's return and how, on that day, Christ will establish justice on earth once and for all. I didn't expect him to instantly believe what I was saying, but I wanted him to see how deeply the gospel addresses the issue of injustice, and why it matters so much.

People today recognize the tremendous importance of justice, and this can lead to opportunities to discuss why divine judgment matters. Judgment Day reveals aspects of God's character that will often surprise skeptics: that God is angered by injustice and unrighteousness, and that he is on the side of the voiceless and defenseless—he is for the abused and oppressed. The opposite of love is not anger but indifference. If God refuses to judge evil, then it means he is complicit in it. As the theologian Miroslav Volf notes, "A non-indignant God would be an accomplice in injustice, deception, and violence" (*Exclusion and Embrace*, page 297).

Our problem is that we want God to right all that is wrong, just so long as his divine justice isn't aimed at us! But we can't have it both ways. A just God who will one day right all the evils of injustice can't be expected to suddenly behave like a benign celestial Santa Claus when it comes to us. The seeds of injustice are ultimately the result of our human rebellion against God, and those seeds have taken root in our own hearts, too.

The Bible assures us that when Judgment Day comes, Christ Jesus will judge all humankind fairly (Romans 2 v 11). What this means for those who have never heard the gospel (or other possible scenarios) is something that only our wise, fair, and merciful God can decide (though it is worth bearing in mind that all of us are undeserving of God's free gift of grace). What the Bible makes clear is that all human beings are sinners and that no one can be saved apart from Jesus having died on the cross for their sin.

And judgment results in consequences. Those who have refused God's offer of grace and tragically insist on living apart from God's presence will, in effect, have their desire granted. Tim Keller writes, "They get in the afterlife what they most wanted—either to have God as Savior and Master or to be their own saviors and masters" (https://www.redeemer.com/redeemer-report/article/the_importance_of_hell, accessed 12/23/19).

While this is hard for people to hear in our age of "tolerance," hell is a reality. God does not want this for anyone, but he will not override our insistence to live apart from his presence. The Bible presents this judgment both as God's sovereign, holy will, as we see in 2 Thessalonians 1 v 9, and also as the choice of human beings. In other words, the door is locked on both sides. Keller puts it this way: "Hell is simply one's freely chosen path going on forever. We wanted to get away from God, and God, in his infinite justice, sends us where we wanted to go."

Yet Christians need not approach Judgment Day with fear. The Judge we will meet is the Jesus who loves us and the One who has died to bear God's judgment for our sin (Romans 8 v 1). It is a remarkable thought that the Judge of all history came to our planet to be judged for our sakes. Because God judged sin in Jesus, when we put our trust in Christ we can live in confident hope because our eternal future is assured. On Judgment Day no one will want justice to fall on them: we will all want what the English sixteenth-century one-time royal favorite Thomas Cromwell begged King Henry VIII for at his execution: "Mercy, mercy, mercy!" Yet mercy is precisely what God offers through the gospel of Jesus Christ, because justice has been satisfied at the cross. We want justice, we need mercy, and the gospel offers both.

WHY JUDGMENT DAY IS SUCH GOOD NEWS

One aspect of God's character that will be seen clearly at Christ's return is the righteousness of God. Because God is righteous, he calls his children to live righteous lives, both on the private and public levels. Demonstrating God's righteousness is a significant part of our witness. If people cannot see Christ's character through us, how will they believe there is a Judgment Day, when a righteous God will right all that is wrong?

The Personal Level

I recently spoke to a conference of American pastors and leaders sponsored by Ravi Zacharias International Ministries. The apologist Vince Vitale noted in his lecture at the same event that we are living in an age where people seem to take offense at everything. It is becoming impossible not to offend people's sensitivities. We are also living in a time when it seems that nothing is forgiven. Witness the popularity of revenge films, the increasing incidences of road rage, and the fact that one of the most popular words used on social media is "unforgivable."

How do we respond to a world where there is so much offense and so little forgiveness? By demonstrating Christ's character through the fruit of the Spirit, especially love, kindness, and forgiveness. There is an ethical, moral aspect to living righteous lives: we confess our sins and depend on the Spirit's power to overcome them. We do not judge others because we know Christ is coming to judge the whole world and he doesn't need our help. We forgive others because one day we will be living eternally with God's redeemed community. We are to be slow to take offense, and very quick to forgive. Living righteous lives has a great impact on our witness, especially in our age of skepticism. Though we are not perfect, the world needs to see in our lives the reflection of the One we claim to follow and love.

The Public Level

Our personal sin isn't the only form of brokenness on our planet. As we've seen, our world, though beautiful, is very broken, and it suffers from the results of sin: abuse, poverty, racism, cruelty, violence, and injustice. These are the very things Christ will erase when he returns.

What difference does knowing that make to how we live today? At the moment, there is a tension between Christians who emphasize proclaiming the gospel and those who focus primarily on justice concerns—so it is necessary to think about this tension here.

Jesus demonstrated tremendous compassion to those who suffered. He fed the hungry, he healed the sick, and he uplifted the marginalized and forgotten. Yet we must not forget that after feeding the five thousand, he said, "I am the bread of life; whoever comes to me shall not hunger, and whoever believes in me shall not thirst" (John 6 v 35). In other words, Jesus met basic human need and then used it to point people to their ultimate need for eternal life in him. He didn't think that meeting physical need was unimportant, but neither did he think that it was sufficient. Jesus didn't separate the ministry of mercy from the ministry of proclamation. But his primary focus was addressing the need for all humanity to find peace with God through salvation: "For what does it profit a man to gain the whole world and forfeit his soul?" (Mark 8 v 36).

Likewise, we are called to minister to the world through both word and deed, because proclamation and mercy are inextricably bound together in the person of Jesus Christ. As the late Sir Frederick Catherwood wrote:

> "The last great commandment of Christ was that it is a Christian's duty to preach the gospel of salvation, the offer of God's forgiveness for our rebellion. Eternal salvation matters more than anything in this life. But the society in which we live does not believe in sin, so it sees no need for salvation. It sees the church as, at best, a cozy club of like-minded people [or], at worst, as a dangerous sect. Words alone are not enough."
>
> (*At the Cutting Edge*, page 214)

We must do our best to heal the injuries and injustices in this world, because all human beings are made in God's image and because Jesus calls us to love our neighbor. Catherwood continued:

"I do not believe that we will win this public argument unless words are backed by deeds and especially by obedience to the second great commandment, to love our neighbors as ourselves. Christ taught the people, but he also healed and fed them. Because he showed his love by his care for their needs, which they felt most acutely, many were prepared to believe him when he told them of a spiritual need which they did not yet recognize. When, finally, he gave his life, thousands were converted. Christians have to follow Christ's example." (page 215)

Our call, therefore, is to display *and* declare the gospel—to show *and* share the kingdom of God to and with those around us. Both are important and both must be done together. The need for people to place their truth in Christ is our primary appeal, but it must be backed up by our actions.

THE RENEWAL OF THE EARTH

When the Bible speaks of Christ renewing heaven and earth at his return, it is not speaking of obliterating this world; it is speaking about the healing and restoration of this world! At Christ's return heaven will come to us! Heaven and earth will be reunited, so that they will no longer be separated as they are now but will be one. It will be so transformed that we can speak of it as "new" replacing "old." Christ will set up God's kingdom on earth:

God's dwelling place is now among his people, and he will dwell with them. They will be his people, and God himself will be with them and be their God.

(Revelation 21 v 3)

This renewal fills us with immense hope and joy because we know that evil doesn't have the last word—God does! Satan will be led to his doom, and God's people will be united to God and to each other, for the old will have gone and the new will have come.

WHY THE NEW EARTH IS SUCH GOOD NEWS

While there are several ways to communicate and demonstrate the relevance of Christ's renewing heaven and earth to unbelievers, there are two things in particular that we must demonstrate.

The Good of God's World

We know that this world isn't all there is and that we were made for a different, utterly renewed one. One day we will live in our true home, the home we were created for and that will satisfy us completely. Yet this very knowledge actually frees us to enjoy the good that this world still offers, for we enjoy them as glimmers of that future home. We are free neither to look to them as our everything, giving us a meaning and security that they cannot; nor as nothing, to be dismissed and ignored.

In C.S. Lewis's *The Screwtape Letters*, the senior devil, Screwtape, chastises his devil-in-training, Wormwood, for allowing his "patient" (the man that Wormwood is seeking to tempt away from God) to enjoy simple human pleasures. Screwtape is worried:

> "You allowed the patient to read a book he really enjoyed
> … to walk down to the old mill and have tea there [and]
> walk through the country he really likes … Were you
> so ignorant as to not see the danger of that?" (page 58)

What Lewis argues through Screwtape is that experiencing real pleasure and real pain in this life actually provides a touchstone of reality that points people towards God. Enjoying this world as we let the goodness in it point us towards our eternal home will bolster our faith as we walk towards that home.

In other words, there is no inconsistency in being a pilgrim who is journeying to the next world and yet at the same time enjoying and appreciating this one. And living this out will greatly strengthen our evangelism because the wider our interests and delights are in this world, the greater the opportunities there will be to naturally connect with unbelievers and to find common ground. When Christians say they don't know how to connect with unbelievers, I usually say, "Start with your natural interests! Sign up for art or cooking classes. Join a tennis club or a golf team. Start a book club with your neighbors. Take language classes or attend a lecture series that interests you. And enjoy them and those who attend!" Finding meaning and beauty in this world is not only a good thing—it can lead to many spiritual opportunities.

Hope in Suffering

We hear a lot about the need for Christians to be vulnerable and authentic, which is true. Being authentic witnesses means we can reveal our tears and our difficulties when we are struggling. Yet the world needs to see more than our vulnerability. People need to know that our confidence and faith in God aren't based on present circumstances but on the beauty, power, truth, and stead-fast character of God seen through Jesus Christ. They need to see that our endurance and resilience in times of difficulty are because we are trusting in the living God.

Bobbie Wolgemuth was a breast-cancer survivor whose cancer returned with a vengeance. When Dick and I visited Bobbie and her husband, Robert, in Orlando, she had been battling the return of cancer for almost two years. She was seated in a lounge chair to conserve her energy while she excitedly told us what God was doing in her ministry to young moms and her tea parties for children—and the significant conversations she was having with unbelievers.

When we were alone in the kitchen, I told her how moved I was by her peace and joy. She said:

> "Of course, there are times of sadness when I think of leaving my beloved husband, our two precious daughters and our beautiful grandchildren. But lately I've sensed Jesus telling me that my time on earth is nearly over. Think of it, Becky! All these years I've poured my heart out to Jesus and loved him so—and soon I will see him face to face! No more barriers. Faith will finally become sight. And on that day when Jesus returns to earth, he will make all things new! No more disease or sorrow or pain. God's redeemed people will live for all eternity in his glorious presence. I can hardly wait!"

What struck us most about Bobbie is how her present suffering was entirely shaped by her certainty of heaven and the future return of her Lord. It not only deepened her capacity to absorb and endure suffering; it made her a passionate witness for Christ. Everyone who met Bobbie—believer and skeptic alike—saw that circumstances hadn't crushed her because she had future hope. And it's in knowing that hope that we learn truly to live. I said to Dick as we left, "We have just been with a woman dying of cancer, yet have you ever met anyone more alive than Bobbie?"

The last thing Bobbie said to me was...

"It's amazing how clear everything becomes when you are close to death. You see that what Jesus offers is what is solid and true and eternal—it is evil that is passing. As wonderful as my life has been, I'm absolutely certain that the life to come will be far more glorious and real than anything I've ever known."

C.S. Lewis wrote of his characters in his final book in the Narnia series, *The Last Battle*:

"All their life in this world and all their adventures in Narnia had only been the cover and the title page: now at last they were beginning Chapter One of the Great Story which no one on earth has read: which goes on forever: in which every chapter is better than the one before." (page 184)

On October 28, 2014, at 62 years of age, Bobbie Wolgemuth began living Chapter One of the Great Story.

Christ's return fills us with a hope and brings us a joy that can't be extinguished by pain, suffering, or grief. That is a powerful witness, and it offers profound hope to those around us who believe that suffering can only ever be a disaster. We can tell them that for those who follow Christ, one day there will be physical wholeness. One day there will be justice. One day there will be renewal. We can have hope because we know how the story ends!

Not only that, but Christ's return gives us a cause to live for—a purpose that makes life worth living for. There are many throughout the generations, but particularly among millennials and Generation Z, who are looking for justice and searching for a cause greater than themselves to make sense of their lives. The cause of living for and speaking about the Christ who will return is the greatest cause there is, and the only one that will make a difference to eternity. Archbishop Benjamin Kwashi, along with his wife Gloria, has endured enormous persecution for his faith in Nigeria. He once said, "This is a gospel worth living for, and it is a gospel worth dying for!"

The greatest source of encouragement we can offer anyone, at any time and in any place, is the gospel of Jesus: the truth that Christ has died, Christ is risen, and Christ will come again. We need to learn to live it and to communicate it as good news. We need to live praying for ourselves the final prayer of the Scriptures (Revelation 22 v 20): *Come, Lord Jesus!*

QUESTIONS FOR REFLECTION

- "A non-indignant God [when it comes to human sin] would be an accomplice in injustice, deception, and violence." How might Jesus' future divine judgment of sin actually be seen as good news to people today?

- "There is no inconsistency in being a pilgrim who is journeying to the next world and yet at the same time enjoying and appreciating this one." Do you tend to forget you are a pilgrim or to forget that we are allowed to enjoy this world? How does emphasizing one truth at the cost of the other adversely affect the way we live, work, and witness?

- If you had three minutes to tell someone the gospel story, what would you say? What would be the key elements you'd include to communicate the story of the gospel? In what ways might you be tempted to tweak the gospel message in order to make it more palatable in your culture?

SECTION THREE:
THE METHOD

CHAPTER ELEVEN

WHY, WHAT, AND WHO

"What image comes to your mind when you hear the word 'evangelist'?"

Several years ago I asked the attendees of an American conference where I was speaking to answer that question. I wrote their answers on one side of a blackboard: "Pushy... rude... intrusive... don't listen... focused on their agenda..."

Then I asked them a second question: "Can you describe in a few words the person who most influenced you to become a Christian?" I wrote their answers on the opposite side of the board: "Loving... listened... not judgmental... took me seriously... looked for the good in me... appreciated my questions... available... hospitable..."

Seeing the contrast of qualities on the board was powerful. Why was their view of evangelists so negative when their own experience had been exactly the opposite?

The words "evangelist" and "evangelism" elicit strong reactions, particularly in the West—not only in the culture but also in the church. The caricature of the guy with a placard shouting on the street corner is how many Christians fear they will be perceived if they attempt to share their faith. In fact, just say the word "evangelism" and Christians often believe it means memorizing a technique to use on a "victim." But techniques do not motivate or inspire us, nor do they build authentic relationships with others.

What this shows us is that we've forgotten what evangelism actually is. The very word stems from a Greek word which means "Good news! Glad tidings!" The book of Acts and all four Gospels are full of thrilling examples of evangelism—and not one of them reflects these negative caricatures that so many of us carry around with us.

We have already seen many examples in this book of how to engage in personal evangelism, but in this final section we will focus exclusively on the "how" of evangelism: specifically, how to share the good news by demonstrating Christ's love; by declaring Christ's truth (particularly to the spiritually closed); and by depending on the power of God (particularly through the word of God).

Before we begin, though, let's take a brief look at the why, the what, and the who—as well as examining some of the reasons why we struggle to share our faith.

THE WHY OF EVANGELISM

The risen Christ commanded his disciples "to go and make disciples of all nations" (Matthew 28 v 18). Notice what Jesus did not say! He did not say, *Go therefore, all you extroverts, all of you with dynamic communication skills, and all those gifted as evangelists, and make disciples. The rest of you, just hang out. Sing some hymns and wait until I return.*

No, the great commission is a command to each one of us. Jesus commands and calls every Christian—from every culture and every nation on earth, regardless of our gifts or personality

"Jesus did not say,
Go therefore, all you
extroverts, and make
disciples. The rest of
you, just hang out."

types—to be his witnesses. The command couldn't be clearer. That is why the early disciples lived and proclaimed the good news everywhere they went. Even when persecution drove them from their homes in Jerusalem, "Those who had been scattered preached the word wherever they went" (Acts 8 v 4). Evangelism isn't an activity limited only to clergy, evangelists, and missionaries. Nor is it limited to those who have been Christians for a while. God has given all believers at all times the amazing privilege and continuing challenge of being sent to be his witnesses.

And when we witness, we are joining Jesus' whole purpose in coming! Jesus described his purpose on earth this way: "The Son of Man came to seek and to save the lost" (Luke 19 v 10). Jesus died for the salvation of the whole world so that all who come to him in faith may live eternally in God's presence. What does this tell us? That God loves us deeply and passionately—that he loved us even "while we were still sinners" (Romans 5 v 8). It is love that compelled God the Father to give his very best—his own Son. It is love that compelled Jesus to come and rescue a planet that was in desperate trouble. It is the love of the Father, the Son and the Holy Spirit that sends us out in mission. So it must be love that compels us to reach outward to others. If God loves the world and his creation this much, then so must we!

However, we cannot give to others what we do not have ourselves. The love that sent Jesus to our planet and to the cross is the love that we need to have grasped and be enjoying ourselves if we are to be effective. We need to fall in love with Jesus all over again, by asking God to rekindle our first love. We need to be reading the Bible every day and allowing God to speak to us. If we desire to reflect the life of Jesus, we need to immerse ourselves in the Gospels, asking God to help us see Jesus with fresh eyes.

We need to be praying and asking God through his Spirit to give us courage, wisdom, and a deeper love for him and for others. The call to evangelism is a call to become inwardly strong yet outwardly focused. Imagine what God can do through people who are ablaze with the love of Christ!

THE WHAT OF EVANGELISM

What is evangelism? In a sense, we have been exploring that question throughout the book. In his seminal work *Evangelism and the Sovereignty of God*, J.I. Packer emphasizes that the essence of evangelism is the communication of the gospel, but without forgetting one salient truth: "Evangelism is man's work but the giving of faith is God's" (page 40). God is the great evangelist and only the Holy Spirit can convict of sins and draw human beings to God.

When we look at how believers engaged in evangelism in the Bible, we see it comprising three things. Evangelism is the act of sharing the good news of Jesus Christ in word (proclamation) and deed (actions) and invitation (calling people to trust Christ Jesus as Lord and Savior). Those three actions—speaking the good news, living the good news, and inviting others to follow Jesus—are essential to biblical evangelism.

Carrie Boren Headington, the Canon Evangelist in the Episcopal Diocese of Dallas, says that evangelism is holding together proclamation, social action, and invitation in the way of Jesus in joy: it is sharing the good news...

"that God is real, God is alive, that God wants to be in a life-transforming eternal relationship with all people, and that this relationship has been made possible through the reconciling action of Jesus Christ." (*Acts to Action*, page 110)

THE WHO OF EVANGELISM

That quote reminds us that God, of course, is the greatest evangelist. Only God can change hearts, open blind eyes, and produce conversion. In Acts 16, when Paul arrived in Philippi, he went outside the city gate to the river, and sat down and began speaking to the women who were gathered there. Among them was Lydia, a dealer in purple cloth, which indicated that she was a successful and no doubt wealthy merchant. She clearly wasn't a woman who lacked confidence, as we see when she persuaded Paul and his companions to stay at her home during their time in Philippi. Paul, Luke tells us, shared the gospel with her, and "the Lord opened her heart to respond to Paul's message" (Acts 16 v 14). In other words, the words were Paul's, but the work was God's. It is God and only God who brings people to faith in his Son—wonderfully, he usually does that life-changing work through his people. We get the privilege of being a part of how God saves people for eternity!

This means two things. First, success in evangelism is not about how many people we convert, since none of us have ever converted anyone! Success is about loving people with our lives and with our words—about showing them Jesus and then telling them the gospel of Jesus in as faithful, engaging, and loving a way as we are able to. We are not responsible for someone's response to the message, but we are responsible for sharing that message. Remember, God is pleased when we witness to his Son, whether the result is conversion or rejection. Rico Tice puts it this way:

"What is successful witnessing? It's not someone becoming a Christian—it's someone hearing about Christ … You have not failed if you explain the gospel and are rejected. You have failed if you don't try."

(*Honest Evangelism*, pages 64, 65)

Second, we must remember that we need God-confidence and not self-confidence. When we know that, as we bear witness, God can work to open blind eyes and hearts to respond to the gospel message, it makes us bold and prayerful. God is with us and is backing us up as we speak. Who knows how he may use our words?

So, start to pray boldly. Ask God to show you where he is already at work in your immediate world—ask him to point you to those in your family, your neighborhood, your workplace, your community, and/or your city who he is preparing to hear the gospel. Begin there—and remember that God may send some of us to the ends of the earth.

SO WHY DO WE STRUGGLE?

In all the years of equipping Christians around the world in evangelism, we have seen that one of the biggest issues that Christians struggle with is fear.

"What if I Offend?"

Think of how many times you have wanted to share your faith but then hesitated because you feared you might offend. So why not share your fears with skeptics? Why not say, "You know, I am truly excited about my faith, and I want to share it with you. But I'm so afraid that I might turn you off that I hesitate"? What does that tell our skeptic friends? That we are not aggressive, overbearing,

Bible-thumping fanatics. In fact, we are normal! We don't want to dump a message on them and run away. We value our relationship with them and we are aware of their sensitivities—in fact, we share them! It is amazing the freedom that we experience when we are simply honest with seekers and skeptics about our own fears—including our fears about sharing our faith!

"What If I Am Rejected?"

Sometimes people reject us because they are under a conviction of sin. They are actually rejecting God, but we get the bullets. There isn't much we can do about that. But sometimes Christians are rejected because we've been too aggressive. That is something we can change by listening carefully, by understanding where someone who doesn't follow Jesus is coming from, and by not barging in with the gospel prematurely. But there is another issue regarding our fear of rejection. We live in very self-focused age. We worry excessively about our feelings, like our fear of being rejected.

What are we going to say to people like the apostle Paul when we meet him in heaven? Here is a man who was flogged, beaten to a pulp, left for dead, bitten by snakes, hated, maligned, and falsely slandered, all for the sake of the gospel (2 Corinthians 11 v 23-28). What will our response be? "Paul, didn't those hostile responses really hurt your feelings? Weren't you frightened? I was, so I kept quiet."

One wonderful thing about Paul's story is that he *was* afraid—even on his second missionary trip! But the risen Christ in heaven came to Paul and said, "Do not be afraid, but go on speaking and do not be silent, for I am with you" (Acts 18 v 9-10, ESV). After that encounter Paul wrote, "Since ... we know what it is to fear the Lord, we try to persuade others" (2 Corinthians 5 v 11).

What did Paul now know? That having fears are normal. The issue is whether we will obey our fears or obey the Lord: or, to put it another way, whether we will be directed by our fears more than by our relationship with our awesome God.

What Paul understood is that the key to overcoming fear is fearing the right thing—because what we fear the most we will serve. So we must place all of our normal, natural fears under the one thing that matters more than anything else: the fear of God. We are to honor and reverence and care about God's approval more than the approval of others because, at the end of the day, only one verdict in life matters: God's!

"What If They Ask a Question I Can't Answer?"

People will ask us questions we can't answer—we can count on it! We need to learn the basic questions that Christians are often asked and get some solid apologetic answers. But what do we do when we don't know the answer?

First, always affirm their question! "That's a good question." "I'm so glad you asked me that." "That's a really hard thing to wrestle with, but it's crucial."

Second, ask for more background, which will give us time to think: "Can you tell me more about that question and why it is important to you?"

Third, pay attention to whether there is emotion tied to the question. A woman asked me with barely repressed anger, "How can there be a God with so much suffering in the world?" I said, "That is probably the most profound and most difficult question of all. But may I ask you something? Am I right that you seem to have a lot of energy around your question?" She answered, "Yes, I do! My mother died when I was ten—so where was God then?" Then I knew that this wasn't an academic question—it was coming from a deep wound of pain. It made a big difference to the way that I answered her.

People appreciate honesty. They aren't expecting us to be able to answer every question. If we say, "That is a tremendous question, and I really don't have an answer. But I would love to research it and get back with you. Is that ok?" what they will see is that we are authentic and honest, and that our faith isn't diminished because we can't answer every question—and it usually causes them to respect us more than dismiss us.

Is sharing the gospel challenging today? Absolutely! But so are the opportunities! The question is, in spite of the challenges we face today, can God use all Christians to be his witnesses? Are we able to engage in a biblical approach that is visual and verbal and invitational—whether people are spiritually open or closed? Can we do so in a way that holds faithfully to the gospel message, while proving compelling and effective in our rapidly changing world? The answer is YES, and YES, and again YES! Which is what we will explore in these next three chapters.

QUESTIONS FOR REFLECTION

- How did thinking about the "who" of evangelism encourage you?
- Which of the questions on pages 177-179 most resonated with you? How did the answer help?
- What comes into your mind when you think of "evangelism"? Why, and what effect does this have on your own witness?

CHAPTER TWELVE

DISPLAYING CHRIST'S LOVE

In the Introduction to this book, I shared my experience of being on a national radio show in the US to be interviewed about evangelism. Afterwards, many listeners from around the country phoned in, all saying that they had family members and friends whom they longed to see become Christians. But they were certain their skeptic friends and relatives would not be interested in engaging in a spiritual conversation. In fact, more than one said that they felt so inept in sharing the gospel that they had prayed and asked God to send someone else who could do it for them!

The interview left me feeling discouraged, particularly since I had just returned from living in Europe, a continent that is far more secular than America and yet where we saw tremendous fruit. So I prayed, "Please Lord, show me if non-Christians are more open to faith in the US than believers here realize."

Soon after the interview I was invited to give evangelism training for an upcoming evangelistic mission that RZIM was sponsoring at a large US university. The story that follows is what happened on my flight out to the event. (I'll tell you what happened on the return flight in the next chapter!)

As I settled into my seat on the plane I met Sue, who was seated next to me. I had work that I had planned to do, but since she was quite chatty and seemed to want to talk, I put away my materials and silently asked God to guide our conversation.

I began by asking questions to learn who she was and to see where we might have common interests. It didn't take long before we discovered that we both liked to travel and learn about different cultures, and that we loved books, jazz, and films.

Then Sue began sharing some of her views, and I quickly realized that we had very different worldviews. (This, of course, is where we often stumble as Christians, because we aren't sure what to say when someone makes a statement we do not agree with.)

At one point in our conversation Sue said, "I really believe in the essential goodness of human nature."

I asked her, "I'm just curious—what do you think about the state of the world? How do you think society is doing?"

"Oh, the world is falling apart. It's a mess!"

"Ok, so help me understand how the world can be a mess when it's filled with entirely good people?"

"That's a very good question!" Sue said. Then she offered this analysis: "I think our problem stems from two sources. People either have addiction issues and need a recovery program, or they are psychologically wounded and need therapy. Don't you agree?"

"I agree that these are real problems and those solutions have helped people," I replied. "But what if we learn to live in recovery from our immediate addiction only to discover that our problem is deeper still? What if our ultimate addiction is to ourselves? What if, at our core, we have a heart problem?"

"I think I may actually agree with you," she answered. "But who on earth has the power to heal an addiction to ourselves? And where do you go for a rehab of the heart?"

"Honestly, I can't think of anyone or anything but God." I said. "In fact, that is what ultimately led me from agnosticism to becoming a Christian—but that's a long story."

"I'd really like to hear your story!" said Sue. And from there, for the rest of the flight we had a significant conversation about the Christian faith.

We landed and as we retrieved our luggage and said goodbye, she suddenly said, "Becky, I feel a bit shy about saying this, but I want to continue our conversation. If I emailed, would you write me?"

I told her that I'd be delighted.

She wrote, and I emailed back, saying at the end of my email, "I told you that I am a Christian, but I didn't mention that I'm an author. One book I wrote is called *Hope Has Its Reasons*, for people who are searching for God or for something they can't quite name. May I send it to you?"

She instantly wrote back saying, "Are you psychic?! How did you know I am searching for God? Please send me your book!" We are now having an ongoing email conversation about Christianity.

Jesus calls all Christians to be his witnesses—so we all need to learn how to share our faith effectively. And Jesus shows us how to put his command into practice: "As the Father sent me, I am sending you" (John 20 v 21). In other words, the very manner in which Jesus was sent must shape the way we go. Jesus doesn't just give us the message of our faith; he shows us the way to share it.

That means we need to pay attention to how Jesus engaged with people and how he talked about faith. Think about it: when God the Father decided to communicate the good news to our planet, he didn't drop fliers from heaven that said, "Smile, God loves you!" He sent his Son—a person. And his strategy hasn't changed. God wants to use us before formulas or techniques. The means of evangelism, first and foremost, is still his people; and the motive for evangelism, more than anything else, is rooted in the love of God for his creation: "For God so loved the world that he gave his one and only Son, that whoever believes in him shall not perish but have everlasting life" (John 3 v 16). The primary motivation for evangelism and discipleship is very simple: it is love.

When a teacher of the law asked Jesus, "Of all the commandments, which is the most important?" without hesitation Jesus said:

> "Hear O Israel, the Lord our God, the Lord is one. Love the Lord your God with all your heart and with all your soul and with all your mind and with all your strength." The second one is this: "Love your neighbor as yourself." There is no commandment greater than these.
>
> (Mark 12 v 29-31)

When our lives bear the stamp of this kind of love—love first of God and then of others—we are reflecting the deepest reality of all existence: the trinitarian nature of God. God is a relational being—Father, Son, and Spirit: three Persons living in perfect, loving harmony with each other. We have been made in God's image, which means we have been created to love. Love is where personal witness begins. Very few people respond positively when they hear the gospel unless they believe that the person they're hearing it from cares about them. In other words, effective personal witnessing happens when those who are hearing about the love of

Christ get a glimpse of that love in the person they're listening to. So, what does it look like to love people as Jesus did?

HOW JESUS ENGAGED WITH THE WORLD

Jesus demonstrated that to relate well to people, we must be radically identified with people in love and yet radically different in holiness. To identify with people is to walk alongside them in solidarity and compassion, just as Jesus did. People in Jesus' day thought holy men could only be found in synagogues, but Jesus' work was often in the marketplace or at the meal table. He had a "go to them," not a "come to me," approach. He went to weddings and parties; he ate meals with people who were considered to be despicable sinners. He expressed compassion by listening carefully to people, asking questions, responding to their need for healing, and always seeking to understand the person he was talking to.

But to identify with others is not the same as being identical to them. If we become identical—if people cannot tell that we are in any way different—we will lose what makes our witness distinctive. Jesus' difference was evidenced by his miracles, by his own holiness, and by the way he was willing to speak uncompromising truth. His identification was seen in his love and compassion towards the forgotten, to the overlooked, and to those who were considered to be lost causes. Our challenge is to go into the world as Jesus did: identifying with people, without compromising our identity as God's people.

Further, Jesus lived life with great expectation because he knew two things. First, he knew that God was always at work and seeking to make himself known. Second, he knew that no matter how far people were from God, all human beings have been created to know and love God.

Our sense of expectation will be greatly strengthened when we remember that God is actively seeking people who cross our paths, that he desires to speak through us, and that people are often more spiritually open than they first appear. It's hard to overestimate the importance of how faith shapes our attitude. If we assume that people will be intrigued to have a spiritual conversation, they quite often are. Conversely, if we are embarrassed and apologetic, and our attitude (if we speak at all) is one of "I know you probably won't find this interesting or relevant," then unsurprisingly people will most often agree.

Let me give you an exciting challenge. Ask God each day, "Show me where you are at work today, Lord. Let me have a conversation about you with someone in my life that you are seeking. Don't let me miss what the Spirit is doing!" This is not only an exciting way to live; it will build your faith and spiritual sensitivity because it will cause you to listen and pay attention to God and to people as you go about your day.

HOW JESUS LOVED

Love Is Authentic and Not Manipulative

Jesus wasn't one person with his disciples and a different one when he spoke to skeptics or critics. To use our modern vernacular, Jesus was authentic. He didn't engage in what we might call "God-talk." He used language that connected with the experiences and concerns of the person he was speaking to. He didn't have a sales spiel or a formula, nor did he say the same thing to every unbeliever he met. In fact, Jesus never spoke the same way twice when he was expressing his message. While the essence of the gospel message was (and is) the same, how he approached people was shaped by who they were as a person.

This is not to say that Jesus did not call for change. Sometimes younger believers tell me, "I try to love people like Jesus did, but I'm not trying to convert them or get them to move from Point A to Point B, because that would mean I have an ulterior motive or an agenda, and Jesus never did."

But Jesus said, "The Son of Man came to seek and to save the lost" (Luke 19 v 10). Jesus did have a purpose, and he went to the cross to sacrificially achieve it. It was not an "ulterior motive," because he never hid it. Jesus' purpose was his longing to see people be reconciled to God. Having a purpose did not mean that Jesus violated a person's integrity, nor does it for us. Living our lives with a godly purpose, which is accompanied by love, is very different from manipulating a person or seeing people merely as evangelistic projects. We long to see people come to Christ, we look for opportunities to rouse their curiosity about faith, and we share our faith when the opportunity arises. We do this not only because Christ commanded us to, but because God loves people and so do we. As Paul put it to a new church in Thessalonica, "We loved you so much that we were delighted to share with you not only the gospel of God but our very lives as well, because you had become so very dear to us" (1 Thessalonians 2 v 8). It is because of God's love that we treat people with integrity and dignity, and it's why we share the gospel message with them.

Love Knows That Everybody Is Somebody

The book of Genesis tells us that all human beings have been made in God's image, which means that all life is precious and sacred.

Knowing this must impact the way we witness—because it did for the Lord Jesus.

One day Jesus was passing through Jericho, knowing that in a very short time he would be dying on the cross for the sin of all humankind. As Jesus walked down the road, a blind beggar, Bartimaeus, cried out to Jesus not once but twice, asking Jesus to have mercy on him by healing his blindness. Luke tells us that "those who led the way" (referring to the disciples) rebuked Bartimaeus with very strong words, telling him, essentially, to shut up (Luke 18 v 39). The implication in their rebuke is *Don't you know who Jesus is? Who do you think you are, interrupting this very important man?*

But Jesus stopped and told the disciples to bring Bartimaeus to him—which must have been rather an embarrassing moment for the disciples! Then Jesus healed the man's blindness, and his new-found sight caused him to follow Jesus, praising God (v 42-43). What was Jesus wanting his disciples to understand? Surely he wanted them to recognize their own blindness: to realize that no human being is insignificant to God. While the disciples regarded Bartimaeus as a man not worth Jesus' time, what Jesus seemed to be saying was *Don't you understand that in a matter of days I am going to die for this man, and for the whole world? Can't you see that everyone is someone to me?* That was a lesson the disciples needed to learn—and so do we!

Love Sees Beyond Appearance

Jesus always looked beyond appearances. He looked for signs of spiritual openness even in the most unlikely people, which often shocked his disciples and the religious community. He didn't assume that a person's immoral lifestyle meant that they weren't spiritually open (John 4 v 18). Likewise, we must look beneath the surface and discover a person's needs and longings—why they look, speak, believe, and act the way they do.

The Samaritan woman that Jesus met in John 4 is a good example. When the disciples came back to the well and saw Jesus conversing with her, they were shocked. Perhaps her appearance suggested a sketchy lifestyle, but even simply speaking with a woman in public was considered highly inappropriate in that culture. The disciples took one look at her and seemed to conclude, "*That* woman? Become a follower of *Jesus*? No way!" But Jesus looked at her and came to the opposite conclusion. What Jesus saw in her going from one man to another wasn't just that she was a woman with loose morals. Her behavior indicated a hunger for God. What Jesus seemed to be saying to his disciples was *Look at how open she is to God. Look how hard she's trying to find the answer to her thirst—yes, in all the wrong places, but she is looking!*

The author and pastor Steve Carter writes that Christians must "live a life that demands an explanation" (*This Invitational Life*, page 32). People should see a love, grace, and joy emanating from us that they want to know more of. We must follow Jesus' model and ask ourselves how we interpret the needs and lifestyle of people we meet. Do we look at their messy lives and say, "That's wrong," and walk away? Or do we take time to get behind the mask and discover who they are by listening to their story?

We must never forget that no one is beyond being redeemed by God's unconditional grace! What an opportunity we have to show people that they are right in wanting to fill the inner void, so that we might share the surprising truth that the emptiness inside is a God-shaped vacuum.

Love Affirms the Good in Others

When Jesus spoke to that Samaritan woman, he asked her to go
and bring her husband.

> "I have no husband, " she replied. Jesus said to her, "You
> are right when you say you have no husband. The fact is,
> you have had five husbands, and the man you now have
> is not your husband. What you have just said is quite
> true." (John 4 v 17-18)

Jesus revealed that he knew her secret, the reason for her deep
shame. In doing so, he not only revealed his divine nature, but he
helped her begin to understand why she so desperately needed what
he was offering. Jesus spoke truth, yet without berating or demean-
ing her—instead he affirmed her twice for being honest when all
she had said was "I have no husband." Jesus was always looking for
legitimate ways to build people up, particularly the downtrodden
and sinful, in order to give them hope—and so must we.

I was teaching at a church when an elderly woman came up
to me and said, "After listening to you, I realized that I've been
doing everything wrong. I don't pray for unbelievers. I don't even
like them, because I don't approve of their behavior. But I've been
so convicted by seeing Jesus' love for the lost. So I've asked God
to forgive me and to help me to not be so judgmental and to do
what Jesus did—to affirm the good I see in unbelievers."

The day after the conference I ran into her, and she said, "Becky,
you aren't going to believe what happened! I was sitting on a
bus this morning when a hippie guy climbed aboard. He had a
Mohawk hairdo and was covered with tattoos. Then he sat down
next to me! I was horrified until I remembered my commitment
to engage in conversations with people very different from me,

and to say something honest but affirming. But I took one look at that man and felt I had nothing to say—until it hit me! Then I said, 'Son, I just want to congratulate you, because I noticed that all your tattoos are spelled correctly. Praise God!'"

Well, at least it's a start!

PUTTING THE "JESUS WAY" INTO PRACTICE

Where do we begin in being a witness for Jesus? First, look at the people God has brought into your life: neighbors, colleagues at work, people at the gym, parents of your kids' friends, and so on. Then think about how to simply build real friendships with them.

I have a younger friend, Missi, who takes seriously Jesus' command to be a witness and to love her neighbors. One day she had an epiphany: "It suddenly occurred to me that I could start reaching out to others by doing what I genuinely love to do, and simply invite others to join me!" Since hospitality is something Missi and her husband love to do, they started from there.

They had just moved into the neighborhood, and since they both love films, they put fliers in their neighbor's doors and invited everyone to join them on their front lawn. It has now become a regular neighborhood activity. Missi says, "These movie nights are such a low-shelf way to gather people for collective joy and to help us get to know each other. Our last movie night we had 89 people come [she has a big front lawn!] because news of fun and good times travels fast, especially when it's free and open to everyone!" It has proven to be a wonderful way to build relationships. After movie nights, their phone always starts ringing with people wanting to get together to talk—and that has often led to their having meaningful spiritual conversations.

At the beginning of the school year, they invite all the parents from their kids' classes to come for snacks and beverages on their front porch. They find inviting parents to a "safe place" gets the ball rolling, and soon people begin to share their challenges. Then it's easy to follow up by inviting someone over for coffee so they can talk at a deeper level. Out of those conversations they may invite new friends to church and lunch afterwards, or invite one or two to a "book club" on one of the Gospels. But here is the key: people come because they know that Missi and her husband genuinely care about them—which is the foundation of all personal evangelism. And, no matter the size of the place you live, and no matter the area God has put you, there will be ways that you can do the same.

RAISING THE TOPIC OF FAITH

So, you've prayed for a genuine, Christ-like love for those around you—and God's answered your prayers. You've worked at getting to know those around you, and you've put yourself out to create genuine relationships. And then... what? One of the questions we are most often asked is "How do we move from a 'normal' conversation to a spiritual one? How can we raise the topic of faith naturally?" We'll look at this more in the next chapter, particularly with reference to people who seem to be spiritually closed. But let's return to the story of Sue, and review and then unpack the conversation. It will help us see how we can introduce our faith to conversations in a natural and organic but not a contrived way.

Pray. When talking to someone, always remember to say a quick silent prayer, inviting God to be present and to guide your conversation.

Find common ground. Being a good conversationalist means looking for areas that you have in common. Obviously, the more interests you have, the easier it will be to find common ground! Furthermore, when someone later discovers that you are a Christian, it becomes much harder for people to put you into a box and dismiss you, because you have already connected with them as a human being.

Ask good questions. Questions have enormous power because they aren't preachy, they reveal that we are truly listening and interested in someone, and they engage people and cause them to think. Look at the Gospels: Jesus was brilliant in the questions he asked. Questions can challenge what someone thinks without sounding aggressive or making them feel defensive. For example, when Sue said she believed people were good, I didn't respond by saying, "How can you possibly believe that when the world is in such a mess?" Instead, I asked her what she thought about the state of the world. I asked this because most people will admit that our world is in trouble, but they don't know why.

Gently challenge someone's worldview with further questions. When Sue answered that the world was falling apart, I gently challenged her first statement by asking, "But how could the world be a mess if people are all good?" Sue didn't respond defensively, perhaps because I had listened to her respectfully and had taken seriously what she was saying, without rushing to share my views or show her where I thought she was wrong.

Agree where you can. When she offered a new analysis—that we are psychologically wounded or we have addiction issues—I agreed with her. I think that this was a critical part of the conversation. If I had said, "No, actually the problem is so obvious: we are sinners who need to repent!" I predict that the conversation would have ended with a loud thud! We need to affirm what we legitimately can, listen empathetically, and try to steer the conversation to God's truth. We can do that as we…

Point to the deeper problem, using the terminology that they have already used in the conversation. I asked Sue, "But what if we learn to live in recovery from our immediate addiction, only to discover that our problem is deeper still? What if our ultimate addiction is to ourselves?" In other words, I expressed the idea of sin but I used her language, since I knew she wouldn't understand what the Bible means by sin.

Then she asked the question that opened the door for the gospel: "Yes, but who has the power to heal the heart? Who offers that kind of rehab?" For the first time in our conversation I mentioned God. I told her that it was this very issue that had caused me to go from agnosticism to eventually having faith in Christ. But I didn't launch into a discussion of the gospel—I simply said it was a long story. This gave her permission to divert the conversation if she wanted to, but it was also an invitation in case she wanted to hear more.

In this conversation (and this certainly doesn't happen every time!) it turned out that not only did Sue want to hear my story, but she was happy to discuss faith for the rest of the flight. As our conversation continued, her questions enabled me to share the gospel naturally. At one point she asked, "Does the Bible say why we are addicted to ourselves?" I said, "Yes, it does. It says, in so many words, that we have a 'God-complex.' We keep trying to be God and to run the show. But we're lousy at being God. In fact, this 'God-complex' is actually what the Bible means by the word 'sin'; we have refused to let God be God, and our refusal lies at the core of all that is wrong with us and our planet."

So, by this stage, I had begun using biblical terminology—but only after explaining it in everyday language. To which Sue said, "Well, I definitely have a God-complex, and it is exhausting! And I agree that I make a lousy god! But as bad as I am at running my own life, I honestly can't imagine living any other way."

I have been surprised by how little pushback I usually receive from skeptics when talking about our God-complex. And I had not been discouraged when Sue had said she couldn't imagine another way to live. The timeline for people coming to Christ may be longer than in times past. Yet I can't count how many people I've known who initially seemed like "impossible cases," yet who later softened and became genuine seekers—and some then became Christians.

CONVERSATION STARTED

What I have seen repeatedly over the years is that many non-Christians actually enjoy having spiritual conversations, which is precisely what the research of Barna and Alpha, and Rick Richardson's excellent book on evangelism, *You Found Me*, have revealed. Even with all the challenges in evangelism in today's culture, I think there is more openness to spiritual conversations than we realize, provided we genuinely care about people, don't treat them as evangelistic projects, listen well, share how God is helping us in our struggles, and ask questions rather than argue with unbelievers. While there is no shortage of information in today's culture, there is a desperate shortage of meaning. Younger generations, in particular, seem to be craving connection and are looking for something (or someone) beyond themselves—for an experience or a cause that is bigger than themselves.

Having positive, effective spiritual conversations is truly possible when we ask God to guide us to the people he is seeking and we invite his presence into our conversations, and when we authentically connect with others and genuinely listen and ask good questions. More than anything else, spiritual conversations are possible when what we do and say reflects the love of Jesus.

QUESTIONS FOR REFLECTION

- "Our challenge is to go into the world as Jesus did: identifying with people, without compromising our identity as God's people." In what ways in the coming week could you try to act like Jesus, as described in this chapter? What will this look like for you? Be as practical as you can.
- Will you pray each day, "Show me where you are at work today, Lord. Let me have a conversation about you with someone in my life that you are seeking. Don't let me miss what the Spirit is doing!"?
- How has this chapter helped you to witness in a way that is authentic and effective? In what ways can you turn evangelism from a project into a lifestyle?

CHAPTER THIRTEEN

DECLARING GOD'S TRUTH

"Truth by definition excludes." (Ravi Zacharias)

It has never been easy to proclaim the gospel as God's truth for everyone, which all need to respond to—but perhaps it is particularly difficult to speak of truth in today's climate. Especially in the West, any statement of absolute truth is often seen as arrogant, intolerant, and politically incorrect; and so what we say is good news is greeted as bad news, or bigoted news, by the influencers in culture. And when something is hard, we often are afraid to even try to do it.

That is why we need a global perspective. One of God's great gifts to Dick and me has been the privilege of ministering around the world. We have seen firsthand the tremendous and varied challenges that Christians face. We have seen that proclaiming the truth of the gospel and living out its implications with integrity and love is the greatest challenge for Christians right around the world.

Some of our brothers and sisters are proclaiming their faith under tyrannical regimes or oppressive governments. Some are communicating the absolute uniqueness of Christ in ancient multi-religious cultures like Malaysia or India. Some are speaking the true gospel where there have been dangerous distortions through the "prosperity" or "health and wealth" non-gospels. I will never forget two Nigerian pastors who have witnessed unspeakable acts of atrocity against Christians in their country saying recently at a conference where we spoke in the US, "We beg you, do not compromise your faith, when we in Africa are dying for ours."

The challenges in the West are real but different. We are encouraged to look inward and follow our hearts when God's word says to look upward and follow his commands. Our assumptions about freedom and happiness cause us to resist anything that we fear might stifle our freedom, especially the notion that God has a rightful authority over our lives—to tell us who we are and how to live. We are living in times that deny the possibility of absolute truth: times when any supposed truth is under suspicion and the validity of gospel truth is either denied or ignored. Yet truth is at the core of the Christian life, and it is also the only explanation for the Christian life. As the missionary and bishop Stephen Neill wrote, "The only reason for being a Christian is the overpowering conviction that the Christian faith is true" (*Call to Mission*, page 10).

Throughout this book I have shared many positive conversations that I have had with skeptics, but not all of my experiences have been positive! Several years ago we were flying home after I spoke at a conference on the east coast in America. I struck up a conversation with a woman seated next to me. She told me she was returning from a science conference, so I asked her questions about her field and how she became interested in science. Well into our conversation, she asked me the purpose of my travel.

When I said I had been the speaker at a Christian conference, a dark scowl covered her face.

"Well, I don't believe anything about Christianity. It is a foolish religion, as all religions are!"

Her hostility was obvious, so I said, "You know, I really enjoy talking to scientists like you, because you believe that truth matters, just as I do. I'm sure you'd reject anything that isn't supported by evidence, and I wholeheartedly agree."

"That's right—and Christianity has no evidence whatsoever to support it!" she said aggressively.

I said, "I'd be interested to know what convinced you that there is no evidence to support the Christian faith, because I was once an agnostic and assumed there was no rational evidence—until I began investigating."

"Look here," she said. "I am an atheist, and I don't need to investigate something so beneath my intelligence as Christianity! Clearly you have never read scholars like Richard Dawkins, or you couldn't possibly believe such garbage!"

"Actually I have read Dawkins and even saw him in a debate. Would you be interested in talking about his objections to faith?"

She wasn't.

I made a few more attempts to engage her, but she only became more irritated and angry. Finally, in an attempt to salvage what had become a disastrous conversation, I changed the subject. But it was too late. She declared loud enough for most of the passengers to hear, "Wouldn't you know I'd have to be seated next to this… Christian!"

I knew Dick had been praying for our conversation, so after we got off the plane I asked him where I had gone wrong. He said, "Honey, I felt so badly for you since we had boarded the plane feeling such joy. But as your conversation progressed I realized that not only was she completely closed spiritually; she seemed to be a troubled person. You were loving and you listened, and in no way did you preach—actually, she was the one preaching! But you needed to stop asking questions. You needed to accept that, at least for now, she was completely resistant to any spiritual conversation." Dick was exactly right.

If you share the truth, sometimes you'll meet a person like this. And, if you are like me, you will need to learn when to stop pushing. Yet, at the same time, we must not run in the opposite direction, so that we assume that in a "post-truth" world everyone will react aggressively to the truth and therefore never seek to share it because we assume no one will want to listen. When approached the right way, many people are open to having a spiritual conversation—though when they are not, we need to know when to stop.

How do we have good conversations about Jesus in a world where some are hostile and yet others are hungry—and we won't know which is which until we start speaking?

REACHING THE SPIRITUALLY CLOSED

The apostle Paul faced a pre-Christian Europe that was pagan, relativistic and pluralistic, much like the culture we live in now. We often think that our culture is the hardest culture that anyone has ever witnessed to, and so we assume that the Bible will not have much to say in terms of witnessing today because it was simply easier back then. But our present post-Christian Western culture is actually closer to what Paul experienced in his pre-Christian society than was the age of "Christendom"—for instance, the Victorian era in the UK or the time of the Revolution in America.

Paul knew the difference between proclaiming truth to those who were brought up with a biblical worldview and those who were not. When he was defending the gospel to Thessalonian Jews, for instance, he piqued their interest with his fierce logic and rational argument, and argued on their own grounds from the Old Testament (Acts 17 v 1-8). In pagan Athens, however, his approach was quite different. Paul cited their own pagan prophets to capture their interest: "As some of your own poets have said, 'We are his offspring'" (Acts 17 v 28).

We need to learn to do the same. We often approach those with no Christian background and try to engage them with arguments that work only in a shared biblical framework—and then wonder why people rarely respond with comprehension or interest.

We also need to keep learning from Jesus—we have seen this before, but it bears repeating. Jesus usually asked questions instead of giving answers, and would tell stories instead of preaching sermons. Thus, he could surprise skeptics in ways that caused them to rethink and re-evaluate their position. For example, when an "expert on the law" spoke with Jesus in order to "put him to the test"—to test Jesus' orthodoxy and to show Jesus that he, not Jesus, had the superior grasp of Scripture — Jesus did not "give him the gospel" (Luke 10 v 25-37). First, Jesus did what he always did—he asked questions. Then Jesus told a story—the famous parable of the Good Samaritan—and so, without a hint of condemnation, he revealed to this "expert on the law" his failure to live according to his own standard of truth, the law.

Questions and stories are more subversive than statements because they can puncture those who feel self-satisfied and proud, as in the case of this expert. Good questions also cause people

"Jesus usually asked questions instead of giving answers and would tell stories instead of preaching sermons."

to become engaged and to think. It puts the onus on them and prevents us (and them, hopefully) from becoming defensive or entangled in arguments, while allowing us to understand the other person's beliefs. Jesus' question to this man was a classic example of pre-evangelism. For us, it is an effective way to discern who is open to thinking about Jesus, and also to plant a provocative seed of doubt in those who are spiritually closed. It may mean that our conversation flows, or that the other person opens up about something nagging away at them, or they simply change the topic—but regardless, we can pray that they will be more open with the next Christian they talk to.

How else can we tell if someone is spiritually open or closed? Here are three steps that may prove helpful.

1. Investigate

When trying to determine whether the person we are talking to is spiritually closed or open, we need to ask ourselves, "Do they seem satisfied with their lives and if so, why? Do they resist faith because of something they already believe (another religion, atheism, Marxism, and so on)? Do they consider faith impossible due to particular objections that they have about Christianity: that there is no rational evidence for faith, that being a Christian means being unintelligent, a racist, or homophobic, and so on?" In other words, we need to ask questions to understand where they are coming from.

2. Stimulate

Once we have an idea of who we are talking to, we are better able to spark their curiosity in faith. To rouse curiosity in faith is a very neglected aspect of evangelism, but it is enormously helpful.

One way is through the art of intrigue—as when Jesus said to the Samaritan woman that if she accepted the "living water" he was offering, then she would never thirst again because the water that he offered would become "a spring of water welling up to eternal life" (John 4 v 14).

Another way to rouse curiosity is by offering evidence to a particular concern. If a skeptic tells you there is no rational evidence to support the Christian faith, then knowing some historical or philosophical apologetics—some ways to defend your faith—will be essential in rousing their curiosity in faith. If a person is more interested in questions of meaning and how faith can make a difference in coping with life, then sharing your own journey of faith may be helpful. In short, we need to use evidence that speaks to that particular person—which means we need to start on their turf, not ours.

3. Relate

Investigating and stimulating are often the necessary pre-evangelistic steps that will enable us to communicate Christ and his message more effectively. That does not mean that we will always have the opportunity to share the gospel in every conversation. Much depends on the openness of the person we're speaking to and the nature of our relationship, and even how much time we have to talk.

Remember that, especially with the spiritually closed, God's purpose in a conversation may simply be to cause them to reconsider their unbelief, or to realize that there is more evidence to support faith than they previously thought, or to leave with a more positive view of Christians than they had before, meaning they will be more open to the next believer God brings their way!

HIS QUESTION HAUNTS ME

In the previous chapter I said that I had asked God, after my radio interview, to show me that American skeptics were still open to the gospel. A week or so later I was flying to give evangelism training to students in Arizona and on my flight out I met Sue—and on my return flight, I met Trevor. He was reading a book, so I didn't engage him in conversation until lunch was served. When I heard him speak to the stewardess, I said, "I always enjoy hearing a Londoner speak English!"

"How did you know I'm from London?!" he asked.

I told him that my husband and I had just spent seven years living in the UK, and we embarked on a fascinating conversation comparing our experiences of living in each other's cultures. We talked for quite some time, and then he asked, "Why were you in Arizona?"

"Because I was speaking at a Christian conference," I said.

"Oh, I'm an agnostic. I have absolutely no interest in talking about spiritual things," he replied.

"That's so interesting, because I was once an agnostic!" I said. I'm just curious to know if your reasons for not wanting to talk about spiritual things are the same as mine once were?"

"Well, I don't want to appear rude, but how do you even know that Jesus existed?" he asked.

"That is an excellent question!" I smiled. "When I began investigating Christianity, I was surprised to discover that respected first-century historians who were not followers of Jesus—like the Jewish historian Josephus and the Roman historian Tacitus—still verified some of the basic facts of Jesus' life."

"Ok—I must admit this is very interesting," he responded. "But Becky, your faith is still based on the Bible. How do you know if the New Testament is even historically reliable?"

I affirmed the importance of his question and said it was something that I had needed to investigate myself. I told him the general criteria that historians have established to assess whether any ancient document is historically reliable. Then I told him why I felt the Gospels measured up to the accepted criteria and how well the gospels fared in comparison with other sources from antiquity.

In my experience, most people do not want to be buried in a sea of evidence unless they are academics or specialists in this area—but they do want reasonable answers.

Then Trevor said, "I can't get over that we are actually having a rational conversation about the evidence for Christianity. I have had Christians talk to me about faith before, but when I press them for evidence, they typically argue on the experiential level, and I dismiss them. So, Becky, how would you summarize the essence of the Christian message? And how did you come to faith?"

Since I knew we were about to land, I could only offer a short version of the gospel and my own conversion story. He listened very carefully, and then he said, "There's something I need to tell you. My wife recently became a Christian. She now takes our children to church, and she prays at meal times, which I have no objection to. My six-year-old son asked me last night, 'Daddy, why don't you ever pray or go to church?'

"Becky, when I laid my head on the pillow last night, my son's question haunted me."

He asked if I would send him books that addressed his questions. We got off the plane and said goodbye, but then he turned back and said, "Please, Becky, don't forget to send me those books."

Remember, this was from the man who initially had said, "I have absolutely no interest in talking about spiritual things!" Despite appearances, he turned out to be a Christ-haunted man who had laid his head on the pillow only the night before, wondering how on earth to answer his son!

I sent him several books, and a month later he wrote back saying, "I've just finished your book *Hope Has Its Reasons,* and I've read the books by Os Guinness and Ravi Zacharias. Now I'd like to talk about the Christian faith at a deeper level. And, by the way, my wife is *overjoyed* that we met!"

Trevor was a linear thinker who wanted to hear rational evidence and an explanation, not my experience. He seemed quite satisfied with his life; he didn't appear to be needy or even spiritually open. It wasn't until the end of our conversation that he dropped the bombshell that he was haunted by his son's question. In all this he was very different from Sue, who was not interested in evidence such as the historicity of the Bible but wanted to talk about issues of meaning: why the planet was a mess and what it means to be human. She was also more interested in hearing experiential evidence than Trevor.

People are different. Therefore, the way we speak to them will need to be different, too. We cannot expect a particular technique or the same list of questions to be a one-size-fits-all solution, especially in a post-Christian, pluralistic society. We will need to be prepared, as the Bible says, "to give the reason for the hope that [we] have" (1 Peter 3 v 15), and we will only be prepared if we are willing to risk them being angry or disinterested about what we say, and if we have listened well enough to know who they are and what they are truly asking.

LEARNING TO FISH

Some of us need to remember that Jesus has called us as his disciples to be "fishers of men"—evangelism is not an optional extra. Others of us, though, need to understand that he did not call us to be "hunters of men"—evangelism is not an aggressive activity! Fishing requires bait, which means we need to throw out intriguing, provocative comments about our faith or about God, to see if they rouse people's curiosity. When we do that, sometimes conversations turn to faith almost naturally... and sometimes they don't. If you find bringing up the topic of faith daunting, you are in good company; most of us do. We worry that we cannot do it without sounding forced or phony. I have found it helpful to think about three different types of conversational questions.

Ask Interest Questions

As you talk with people, first discover their interests. Are they interested in politics, sports, music, or issues pertaining to their jobs? If they are retired, do they find pleasure in gardening, being more involved with their grandchildren, or traveling to places they always wanted to see? This is not only about discovering what their interests are but why these activities bring them such happiness. These two kinds of question (what and why) are so natural that we often ask them without even thinking about it.

Ask Opinion Questions and Then Issue Questions

People often tell me that they do not know how to move beyond a superficial conversation to a more significant discussion: for example, how do you move a conversation about sports into a conversation about God?

There are two types of questions to ask, but these are ones that we often miss. First, you can ask people what their views are on a particular topic. Everyone has beliefs—whether they're about politics, favorite sports teams, or the meaning of life! Perhaps you come from a culture where people tend not to share their views or opinions readily—but in these settings, genuinely asking someone for his or her opinion actually communicates respect. So even if it feels initially uncomfortable, this approach is worth a try.

Here are some examples of questions that reflect current issues in America, but the principle can be applied to any cultural context: "You love sports, so I'm curious to know what you think about that sports hero who was caught doping?" Or "Since your children/grandchildren are about to go to university, what do you think about the students protesting to get the administration to dis-invite public speakers who do not share their ideology or beliefs?" Or, "As a lawyer, what's your opinion of that celebrity who didn't go to trial when all the evidence suggested he was guilty of the crime?"

It is in this area of beliefs that conversations can break down. Meaningful interaction can be difficult if our opinions are not shared. Conversations can degenerate into an argument (though only if we let them—it does take two to make an argument!) Our temptation at this stage is to say, rather than to ask. How do we avoid the impasse? By asking a second question: an issue question.

For example, when people complain that they fear the younger generation are becoming "snowflakes" because they cannot handle anyone disagreeing with them, we could ask, "Where do you think this inability to deal with people who have different ideas comes from? How can we learn to live with our deepest differences?" Or, when people complain that "justice" is often visited upon the poor but the rich tend to get away with their wrongdoing, we could ask, "Do you think the old adage is still true—that we reap what we sow? Do you think anyone can escape justice for eternity?"

Dick was recently speaking to a man who enthusiastically shared his love of golf. As they both talked about their love for the game, the man said, "My work is very high pressure, and golf has been a tremendous outlet for me, most of the time." Dick asked, "So what do you do when golf doesn't relieve the pressure?" Attempting to sound jovial, the man answered, "Oh, I guess I try not to drink too much booze." Dick said, "You just hit on the key issue. Can we find something that relieves the pressure but that doesn't trade one problem for a worse one?" To which the man said, "Have you found anything that works?"

Ask a "God" Question

Once we have engaged in this kind of conversation, it is often easier than we think to raise a God question—a question that gets people to engage with their own worldview and consider what difference God would make to this topic.

Let me give you one example. Joe is a Christian and a surgeon. In talking with Sam, another surgeon who wasn't a believer, Joe chatted about their shared interests: what drew him to medicine in the first place? They talked about their views on various issues that were being discussed in the medical community. Then Joe raised the issue question: "I don't know about you, but I've found the most difficult aspect of our work is dealing with patients who are dying. Have you found a way to give hope to your patients who are terminal?"

Sam answered that it was, by far, his greatest challenge. Then he asked Joe if he had found anything helpful, which led to a discussion about God. Joe answered, "After seeing some patients die, I realized what a difference faith seemed to make in how some patients handled death. So I began asking myself, 'What if this life isn't the only life and there is another life that awaits us? What difference would it make to know there is a God who can offer hope in the most dire circumstances?"

Sam asked, "So what did you discover?" Joe then shared his spiritual journey and how he had eventually become a Christian. A few days later, Joe's friend Sam phoned him, asking if they could meet for coffee and continue their conversation. Many more conversations later they met for a Bible study on the person of Jesus, and eventually Sam became a Christian.

In our training conferences we often divide people into pairs or small groups, and ask them to write down the name of a person they want to reach for Christ and what that person's particular area of interest is, if they know it. Then we ask them to write three questions: an "interest" question, to discover peoples' interests and why they find them so enjoyable, an issue question that genuinely relates to their interests, and finally a God question.

Here is what we often hear from people who have attended our conferences or who have seen *Empowered,* our evangelism-training films:

> "I've always felt so inept at raising the topic of faith. But now I'm beginning to understand the art of conversation. I've found that raising a deeper question that is based on what my skeptic friends are truly interested in can more naturally lead to conversations about God. It's certainly a more natural, organic approach than

artificially asking, 'So, by the way, what do you think about Jesus?'"

This isn't about coming up with a new memorized technique or thinking of the perfect questions to ask. It's simply learning the type of questions that take a conversation to a deeper level. The key is that our questions must come from a genuine interest in the person. It isn't a technique or a gimmick. Nor does it mean that we will go neatly from the interest question to the issue question to the God question all in one conversation. We may have several conversations just listening to our friend's interests! Conversations, like relationships, don't work like gear shifts on a car. As we seek to set the overall direction, they progress at their own pace.

PUSHING THE LOGIC

Another way to engage with people who look (and turn out to be) spiritually closed is to push them to consider the consequences of their views. This is not about proving them wrong so we can win the argument. (There is a reason why, straight after telling Christians to be ready to give a reason for the hope we have, Peter says, "But do this with gentleness and respect," 1 Peter 3 v 16.) This approach involves taking people seriously in terms of what they say and what they believe, and then pushing them towards where that leads. In other words, can they live their beliefs in real life, not just in their heads? Os Guinness makes the insightful point in his excellent book *Fool's Talk* that we must look not only at people's beliefs but also for the "treasures of their heart"—the things that are deep in the center of their lives that they profoundly care about (page 123). What our heads believe often comes into conflict with what our hearts cherish.

Years ago, upon returning from studying in Spain, I decided to finish my final undergraduate year in my hometown, at the University of Illinois. I was informed that I would have to take a first-year biology course that I had somehow missed. My biology professor was well-known on campus for being an outspoken atheist. When he discovered I was a Christian, he delighted in baiting me. He began every lecture by saying, "Human beings are nothing more than meaningless pieces of protoplasm—a fortuitous collection of atoms in a universe where chance is king." One day after making these remarks he said, "So let's ask Becky, our resident Christian, what she thinks of my remarks!" I answered in his same friendly banter, "Well, I guess I feel a little sorry for your wife!" He said, "Ah, class, what Becky is asking is whether I can apply my beliefs to my wife, and the answer is: Yes! Absolutely."

On the last day of class, he looked uncharacteristically low and had none of his normal bravado. He began writing on the board but suddenly put the chalk down and said, "I don't think I can teach class today. My 16-year-old daughter disappeared last night. She left a note saying she had been having an affair with a much older man and they decided to run away together. The police are trying to find them in order to bring her back. But I am devastated. She is my cherished daughter, and this experience will scar her for life."

Then to everyone's amazement he said, "So, Becky, what would a Christian have to say to me at this moment?"

"I would like to talk to you privately if I may," I answered, "but not in front of class."

To which he replied, "No! I've been straightforward about my beliefs, so you must tell me where you think my beliefs are in error."

So I answered softly, with tears in my eyes, "I am more sorry for your pain than I can possibly say. But if your beliefs are true, then one thing is certain: a meaningless piece of protoplasm cannot scar."

He answered sadly, "Touche! Class, do you realize what Becky is saying? She is saying that if my beliefs are true, then I should be able to live them out. But I cannot. Not when it comes to my cherished daughter. She is not a meaningless piece of protoplasm, not to me, not ever! Class dismissed!"

I went up to his desk afterwards, and he knew I wasn't coming in a sense of triumph but in profound sadness. He said with extraordinary candor, "Becky, for me to maintain my beliefs in light of the revelation that I can't live them out means I am a fraud. But it's too late for me to change. I can't turn back."

"But it's not too late!" I said. "You are one of the most intellectually honest people I've ever met. You have just courageously admitted that you cannot live by your beliefs. So wouldn't it be reasonable to at least explore an alternative view?"

"Even if there is a God, he would have no interest in me," he said.

"You are so wrong! God loves you!" I answered. "It's why he put me in this class—so that I could tell you this. It is never too late to turn to him!"

Those were our last words. I never saw him again, though I prayed for him and his daughter for years.

It is incredibly painful when people choose not to believe. We have to accept that that may happen, and that it will hurt when it does—but we cannot stay silent when the gospel is a matter of life and death. We must also never stop praying for those who have said no, for "no" does not necessarily mean "never." At the end of the day, we can only leave salvation where it belongs—in the hands of God—and remember that he is pleased by our faithfulness and love.

Evangelism, of course, is glorious when we see human lives transformed. We have explored several ways to introduce faith into a conversation, and we've seen that some people will respond positively and thoughtfully, as Trevor did. So why not give it a go and use one of the approaches that we've looked at in the last couple of chapters? What I have seen again and again is that people are more open to engaging in spiritual conversations when they sense our genuineness and love, and when they see there is sound evidence for our faith. And our authenticity makes them willing to overlook our awkwardness and even our mistakes.

We have seen in the last two chapters that effective biblical evangelism must involve demonstrating Christ's love and expressing God's truth. And there is something else it must involve: the power of the Holy Spirit.

QUESTIONS FOR REFLECTION

- "Jesus usually asked questions instead of giving answers, and would tell stories instead of preaching sermons." Why is this an effective way to begin to engage with people on a spiritual level? How could you adopt this approach next time you are talking about Jesus?
- Think about the people you often have conversations with who are not Christians. How could you start to ask them the types of questions laid out on pages 208-212? What needs do they have, and how would the gospel meet what they feel is lacking in their lives?

- How has this chapter helped you to witness in a way that is authentic and effective?

CHAPTER FOURTEEN

DEPENDING ON THE SPIRIT'S POWER

There is much talk today about our need to be cutting edge and relevant in communicating the gospel. But that does not mean we have to change it. As Simone Weil, the French philosopher, famously pointed out, to be and stay truly relevant we have to say what is eternal. So we must avoid these two temptations: to focus on our abilities or lack of them, or to make the gospel so acceptable to our culture that our message becomes indistinguishable from it. Instead we need to speak and share what is eternal because that is where the power of God is found.

Paul reminded the Thessalonians, "Our gospel came to you not only in word, but also in power and in the Holy Spirit and with full conviction" (1 Thessalonians 1 v 5). Paul is saying that what makes our witness effective is having confidence in the power of God's word—in the message of the gospel as God's Spirit works powerfully through the news about God's Son.

THE POWER OF THE WORD

But how can the word of God be a means for witness to skeptics who do not accept its authority? I think back to my own experience. If someone had asked me what I thought of Jesus in my agnostic days, I would have said that Jesus was kind, gentle, and the type of person everybody loved, especially your grandmother. I accepted this caricature because I had never read one page of the Bible, and because this was how I had seen Jesus portrayed in Hollywood films and religious art.

Then one day I bought a Bible and I began reading through the Gospels.

Instead of finding the harmless, sweet Jesus I had expected, I discovered a man of profound passion who went about casting out demons and saying things like *I've come to set the earth on fire!* He was an extraordinary being who threw furniture down the steps of the Jerusalem temple because of his indignation over religious hypocrisy. The first time I read that story in John 2, as an agnostic, I remember thinking, "I can't believe Jesus is as upset with religious hypocrisy as I am. I never imagined that we had so much in common!"

We discover a lot about people when we learn who likes them and who doesn't. I was stunned to see that Jesus' main detractors were the righteous, respectable religious establishment, while prostitutes, lepers, and other outcasts loved him!

My experience of encountering Jesus in the Gospels not only led to my conversion; it shaped my understanding of what makes for effective evangelism. As an agnostic, I did not believe that what I was reading was the word of God; yet I nevertheless experienced its power. It made me realize the importance of looking at the person of Jesus with skeptics. To put it another way, we need to let Jesus introduce himself to those whom we'd love to meet him.

GET IT OPEN

What I have seen through the years is that once friendships with unbelievers are established and there is a freedom to discuss spiritual issues, a great next step is to invite them to take a deeper look at Jesus. One way to do this is through what I call a "Seeker Bible Study." (Call it whatever seems appropriate for the people you're inviting.) This is not a study for Christians but for people who may be atheists or agnostics, or from other religions, or raised with a church background—anyone who may not be sure what they think about Jesus.

We invite them to come to a neutral place (our home, our school dorm, at the back of a restaurant) to look at one of the Gospels and examine the life of Jesus. We tell them that they don't have to believe in God or believe the Bible is the word of God. We simply invite them to "come and see" and to think of it like a book club. For those with a church background, we might say that this is an opportunity to take a fresh look at Jesus from an adult perspective. The atmosphere is fun and relaxed. After a bit of social time and maybe some refreshments, we facilitate the discussion by asking questions about the Bible text (possibly using a Seeker Bible Study guide), and the conversation begins.

I have found this tool to be effective worldwide, because it isn't a slick program or a gimmick but is based on relationships. We're not inviting strangers but friends. People who wouldn't darken the door of a church feel much more comfortable coming to the home of a friend to spend time with people like themselves—people with lots of unanswered questions. We provide a safe place for people who may never have read the Bible or whose understanding of Christianity is sketchy or confused. It can be done one on one or in a small group (any size is fine, though not more than eight). The reason that the majority of the group must be seekers or skeptics is because nothing kills a "seeker study" faster than having too many Christians! My rule of thumb is that if a Christian wants to come, then he or she must bring a non-Christian.

Another reason the people we invite respond well to this kind of setting is because the gospel is not being taught so much as explored through questions. The format is conversational rather than confrontational—the truth is presented through stories, not a sermon.

The truth is that while some may have been turned off by religious organizations like the church, many are still curious about Jesus. Who was he? What was he like? What did he say and do? Apart from authentic friendship and prayer, I believe the greatest shortcut to evangelism is focusing on the person of Jesus, because Jesus is irresistible! Whether people become Christ-followers or not, I have seen even the most cynical feel drawn to Jesus, which creates room for future discussions.

Why is looking at Jesus so powerful? Because Jesus is so much more than four points of a gospel summary! Jesus is delightful, exasperating, and so different from what most people assume. Think about it: when ordinary people met Jesus in his day, they were amazed by his miracles, astonished by his teaching, shocked by his claims, moved by his tenderness to outsiders and outcasts, and stunned by his criticism of the religious. Jesus always astonished and broke people's stereotypes, and he still does today. That is why evangelism, at its core, isn't about techniques or formulas. It's about bringing people into the presence of Jesus.

We have seen Seeker Bible Studies started in nearly every country where we have ministered. Often we get letters from people after

"While some may have been turned off by religious organizations, many are still curious about Jesus."

we've been in their country. A Chinese woman wrote to me that she was using *Uncovering the Life of Jesus*, my Seeker Bible Study from the Gospel of Luke, with her professional colleagues:

> "The people came because they trust me. We were already friends, and they'd become curious about my faith. These are people who had never read one word of the Bible and knew almost nothing about Jesus. But we Chinese love a good story! What fascinated me most was how Jesus became alive to them. They commented on their surprise in seeing how relevant these Bible stories were to their own lives. Several in the group have now given their lives to Christ."

A microbiologist in Italy invited her research colleagues to come to her apartment for pasta and a study on "Who is the Real Jesus?" using my Seeker Bible Study from the Gospel of John, *Discovering the Real Jesus*. Most of them were atheists but, as they were also fellow research scientists, she had initiated many conversations with them on science versus faith, "new atheism," evolution, and so on. What drew them to come was their respect for her, her obvious love for them, the fact that she took their questions seriously, and her irrepressible joy. She wrote us after the first series ended to say that the most vociferous atheist of the group had just committed his life to Christ.

When we lived in the UK and ministered throughout Europe, we divided our time between working with churches and university student ministry. I will never forget a conference where 1,200 university students came from all across the UK, sponsored by a student organization called UCCF. I thought the students would be hesitant to start a Seeker Bible Study because it was a new idea to most of them. I had just written a new Seeker Bible Study in Luke (which at that point was simply called *Uncover*) and to our astonishment, they loved the idea! By the end of school term, there were over a thousand Seeker Bible Studies happening across the UK, and a tremendously encouraging number of students gave their lives to Christ. We are thrilled that Seeker Studies are now part of the DNA of that whole student movement!

Another Seeker Bible Study has been held in inner-city Chicago in a halfway house for men who have been living on the streets or who have recently been released from prison. They used my *Discovering the Life of Jesus*, and I was fascinated to hear what drew them to Jesus. "They see in Jesus someone they can identify with," the study leader told me. "The authorities don't like him; the religious leaders taunt him about being born out of wedlock; he has no place to lay his head at night; and he befriends prostitutes and lepers. The marginalized people love him, and he loves them."

How could reading Bible stories about a man who lived 2,000 years ago be relevant to people today who live in such vastly different cultures and parts of the world? Because true spiritual power lies in utilizing God's resources: his word and his Spirit. The Spirit of God works through the word of God to reveal the Son of God. That is the reason that a Seeker Bible Study is effective—it is centered in authentic relationships, while at the same time utilizing the power of God's Spirit as his word is opened.

One of my fears is that the world looks at Christians from a distance and concludes that Jesus' primary task is to help us have devotions and to keep us from swearing. But when they encounter the biblical Jesus, they realize that this Jesus would never flee from someone struggling with a sexual addiction, substance abuse, or an eating disorder. And Jesus also has something to say to the successful and seemingly satisfied because they too are often looking for meaning—be they a Jewish religious leader like Nicodemus (John 3) or a successful businesswoman like Lydia (Acts 16).

The Bible shows us that Jesus does not walk away from people because they have problems. Sometimes Jesus gives people a challenge to consider when they don't want to face their problem, like the rich young ruler—but he always loves them (Mark 10 v 21). Jesus is willing to wade in and love us where we are. Most people can't imagine a God who is willing to become deeply involved in our messy lives. So our task is to emulate Christ, to show those around us who Jesus is through the Scriptures, to share the gospel, and to reveal how he has mended our own brokenness and forgiven our sins.

THE WORD OF GOD DOES NOT NEED OUR DEFENSE

God's word is powerful as his Spirit works through it. So we do not need to leap to the Bible's defense. I once heard a Christian in a Seeker Bible Study, in response to a member of the group wondering aloud about something in the passage we were studying, say in a this-ends-this-discussion tone, "The Bible is the divine, inerrant, authoritative word of God." But people coming to a Seeker Bible Study do not need to believe anything in order to come, and once there they need to be allowed to ask questions, wonder aloud, and feel free to pose their objections. (And, as a side-note, using "God-talk" in this kind of setting is unhelpful, because seekers won't understand those words anyway). C.H. Spurgeon put it wonderfully well:

"Suppose a number of persons were to take it into their heads that they had to defend a lion, a full-grown king of beasts! There he is in the cage, and here come all the soldiers of the army to fight for him. Well, I should suggest to them … that they should kindly stand back, and open the door, and let the lion out! I believe that would be the best way of defending him, for he would take care of himself; and the best 'apology' for the gospel is to let the gospel out."

("Christ and His Co-Workers," spurgeongems.org/sermon/chs2467.pdf, accessed 12/23/19)

He is right. In all the years I have been in Seeker Bible Studies, I have seen how mysteriously and powerfully the Bible speaks to all who gather to study it. The Bible has an authority that is undeniable.

JESUS COMES ALIVE

We have done training in Asia, Australia, North and South America, the Middle East, India, Europe, and Africa. What we always hear from those who have led Seeker Bible Studies is how the truth about Jesus seems to leap off the pages and come alive! We hear how amazed unbelievers are by the relevance of these ancient stories to their lives. Often Christians tell us, "It is almost as if Jesus is doing all the work for us!"

That means that anyone who has put together a Seeker Bible Study group can relax. They usually fear that those who come are eager to bite their heads off when in fact they are usually fascinated by the person of Jesus and are surprised by the relevance and the humanity of the stories.

Another reason why seekers respond well in this kind of setting is because the truth about Jesus is not taught but explored through questions. The investigation is conversational rather than confrontational. Truth is presented through story, not a sermon.

And because of this setting, everyone gets to learn from the word, and from everyone else's insights into it—including believers. I was leading a study for women when one seeker asked, "Why do you think Jesus hugged the leper?" One of the few Christians present (one who clearly had not grasped the ethos of the gathering) answered, "Oh, Jesus wasn't worried! He couldn't contract leprosy, since he was the Son of God." Then the seeker said, "Well, I am 40 years old, and this is the first time I have ever read the Bible. I don't know if Jesus is the Son of God, but from what I've seen of Jesus thus far, I think he'd be willing to risk contracting leprosy if he thought he could help that poor man."

Which of these women came closer to understanding the true nature of Jesus? The believer who said there was no risk for Jesus, or the seeker who stated, without realizing it, something close to the doctrine of atonement: that Jesus became sin for us so that he could pay the price for our sins and offer us forgiveness and a new life (2 Corinthians 5 v 21)?

What moved me deeply was when the Christian woman said to me afterwards, "God really convicted me in the study today. I saw how quickly I dismissed that woman's question, which is something we never see Jesus doing. And I realized that her answer may have been closer to the truth than mine! I have so much to learn."

Remarkable things happen when we study the word of God with others. All of us are changed because the word of God convicts everyone! The power of the word and the power of the Spirit bring a new reality into being—a new way of seeing God and a new way of seeing ourselves. With God's word opened, through the power of the Spirit, Jesus comes alive.

LEAVING HOME AND COMING HOME

The wonderful thing about Jesus is how he reaches so many different kinds of people. When we read the Gospels carefully, we find him presenting himself in so many different ways, because the people to whom he was speaking had different characters and stories. To the Samaritan woman he offered "living water"; to Nicodemus Jesus said he had to be "born again"; to those he had miraculously fed with a few loaves and fishes he called himself the "bread of life."

Following Jesus' example means we need to pay attention to what the seekers in our lives are searching for and show them how Jesus addresses what they are looking for. We need to ask ourselves:

- What do our non-Christian friends feel they are lacking in their lives? What are they looking for?
- Are there Bible stories that they would find especially relevant?
- Which biblical pictures or descriptions of Jesus might especially connect with them?

Let's take one picture of Jesus' purpose in coming to earth—to bring the homeless home. The night before he died, Jesus told his disciples:

> My Father's house has many rooms; if that were not so, would I have told you that I am going there to prepare a place for you? And if I go and prepare a place for you, I will come back and take you to be with me that you also may be where I am. (John 14 v 2-3)

The Bible tells us that when we come to Christ "you are no longer foreigners and aliens, but fellow citizens with God's people and members of God's household" (Ephesians 2 v 19). I have met many people who struggle with issues of abandonment and anger from experiences they had as children. No matter how much good in life they experience, they are always waiting for the bad to happen. They feel like orphans in a world that isn't safe. The biblical story in Luke 15 of the prodigal son reveals God's love and desire for reconciliation and relationship.

And this wonderful theme in Scripture is a compelling way to communicate the hope and the power of the gospel to someone who has abandonment issues.

I wrote earlier that on our first day in France, Raphael, Dick, and I asked God to lead us to people that he was seeking. The very next day the manager of the flat that we had rented for our first week came to see if everything was satisfactory.

Martha is sophisticated, bright, articulate, and full of fun. We had talked for several minutes when she asked, "So why are you here in France? For holiday or work?" I said, "Can you stay for a coffee and I can tell you?" As we sat down with our coffees, I began asking her questions about her own life, feeling it was premature to explain the purpose of our trip.

Martha's life was fascinating. She had lived all over the world, working in hospitality. At one point she happened to pull out a cross that she was wearing around her neck. I commented on how beautiful it was, and she said, "You know, I have never worn a cross in my life. I just bought it recently, and whenever I wear it—I don't know how to describe it—I feel a kind of peace, or maybe a sense of protection. I don't know what to make of it."

A little later she said, "Ok, Becky, I never reveal this much about myself to someone I've only just met! But it's unusual to find someone so genuinely interested in me and who makes me feel so comfortable. Now, tell me, why are you and Dick in France?"

When I told her that we were there to speak to churches throughout Provence, her eyes widened and she said, "Well, you can't be a nun since you're married. How on earth did you get into this line of work?" Then I shared some of my story and how I came to faith in Jesus.

She sat in silence for a few seconds and then said, "I am stunned that you are telling me this because yesterday I went to the funeral of a friend. I can't remember the last time I was inside a church. But as the service proceeded, I silently said, 'I don't know if I am addressing God or these four walls, but if you're there, here is my question: Will I ever find the peace I am seeking? Will I ever feel like I've come to my true home?' And now, less than 24 hours later, I meet you! Would you be willing, Becky, to meet me for a meal so we can talk more about these issues?"

The next week we met for lunch in a restaurant. She told me that her parents had both died when she was a teenager, and ever since she had felt abandoned and alone in the universe. She said, "The world has never felt like a safe place for me. But when I said those things in church, almost as a kind of prayer, and the next day I meet you... I wonder if it was not a coincidence that we met?"

"No, it isn't a coincidence," I said. "God heard your prayer, Martha, and it's why we met the very next day. This is God's doing." As we spoke, I was able to share the gospel: God's wonderful purpose in creating us, what went so terribly wrong, how Jesus came from heaven to die for our sins, and how he was raised to life so he could offer us a new life and a new beginning with God.

Then she said, "When I left home all those years ago, it broke the hearts of my remaining family members. But I was so angry and hurt. I was certain God had abandoned me. All my life I have felt disconnected from my true home."

"Martha," I replied, "that is why Jesus came: to bring us to our true home in God. Jesus tells a story in the Bible about an angry son who left home like you did. After experiencing great difficulties he finally returned home. But he was afraid of how his father would respond. How do you think the father responded when he saw him?"

"Well, the son must have broken his father's heart," she answered. "So maybe the father kept him at a distance at first, in order to see if the son was truly sorry?"

"That's exactly what the son thought his father would do!" I told her. "But when the father saw his son walking towards home, he ran to meet him and embraced him. He dressed him in new clothes and threw a huge 'Welcome Home' party for him. That is what God is like, Martha. He loves you, and he has been seeking you."

"What is the next step as far as God is concerned? What did you do to become a Christian?" she asked.

"I told Jesus that I believed that he is the Son of God, who died on the cross for my sin," I replied. "And I thanked him from the heart. Then I said, 'I'm sorry,' and I confessed my sins, especially the sin of running my own life. And I asked him to forgive me. Then I asked him, 'Please come into my life, Jesus, as my Savior and Master.' It was so simple, and yet it changed my life forever."

Tears were now filling Martha's eyes.

"I don't think I have ever felt this much love—but I need to think about this some more and start reading the Bible," she said. "Are there more stories in the Bible like the one you told me?"

I assured her there were! When we said goodbye, she said, "Becky, will you stay in contact with me while I am on this journey?" I assured her that I would, and we have been in contact ever since and are planning on seeing each other on my next trip to Europe.

WE LACK NOTHING

There are two kinds of people in the world: the found, and those who haven't come home yet. The apostle Peter, in reflecting on why the Lord Jesus has not yet returned to bring history to a close, said:

> The Lord is not slow in keeping his promise, as some understand slowness. Instead he is patient with you, not wanting anyone to perish, but everyone to come to repentance. (2 Peter 3 v 9)

God's desire is that no one refuse his offer of grace, though tragically some will. But this verse enables us to understand our place in history. We are living between two of the most life-changing events to occur on our planet. We are living after Jesus came from heaven to earth and before Jesus returns again to bring heaven to earth. What is the significance of God placing us here at this particular juncture in history? It is so that we can join God in his quest to love, seek, and invite people to come home to God! And he has given us all we need: his power through the Holy Spirit in our lives, his truth through his word, and his love through Jesus.

What we desperately need to recover today is a renewed confidence in God and gratitude for the fact that he has given us all we need to reach the world. Even in our poverty and weakness, we lack nothing—because the Lord of lords and the King of kings delights in working his glorious strength through our weakness!

We must be true to our Lord and committed to reaching the hearts and minds of our post-Christian generation. We must be witnesses in all that we say and do in a way that is worthy of the Lord, who was, and is, and is to come.

We have the glorious opportunity to let Jesus be known to this world. Let us go forth with our arms outstretched and our hearts open, knowing that Jesus' love and grace accompanies us every step of the way. What are we waiting for?

QUESTIONS FOR REFLECTION

- Is there someone (or a group of several people) you could invite—or pray about inviting—to open up a Gospel with you and look at Jesus together? What might hold you back?
- Think about a seeker who you know fairly well, and then answer the questions on page 227 with them in mind. How does this help you to think through how you might speak to them about Jesus?
- "And surely I am with you always, to the very end of the age" (Matthew 28 v 20). God has given you everything you need to be an effective witness (his power through the Holy Spirit, his truth through his word, his love and the gospel through the person of Jesus, and the knowledge that you are never alone). How will knowing this truth strengthen you in your evangelism?

CONCLUSION: OUR CRITICAL MOMENT

We are at a critical moment in Western Christianity. Today our culture is increasingly post-Christian: not merely not Christian, but set *against* Christianity. More and more, we are in danger of losing our confidence in the idea that talking about Jesus will make any difference. Yet our secular society leaves people searching for something that gives meaning and purpose to their lives. These are difficult times to stay salt and keep witnessing— and these are the best times to be a witness because the need is so great.

The challenge before us is this: will we, in our post-truth, post-Christian culture, reclaim our confidence and conviction in the God who speaks and acts and who is, as C.S. Lewis said, "the transcendental Interferer?" Will we shake off our timidity before our culture and refuse to be silent, while remaining sensitive to our culture's concerns and thinking hard about how to present our faith in a way that resonates with those we are speaking to? Will we show the world, not in a triumphalist or pushy manner but by word and deed, that receiving Christ as Lord makes all the difference—the only truly lasting difference—in our individual lives, our cities, and our world?

WITNESS IS NOT WITHOUT COST

Jesus warns us that being a witness is not easy or without cost. The Greek word for "witness" is martyr, and the first witnesses for the gospel were prepared to pay with their lives to be faithful. Most of us in the West have not personally experienced this, but many of our brothers and sisters around the world have.

A couple of years ago, I was one of three speakers at a conference for Christian leaders in Wales. Ajith Fernando, from Sri Lanka, spoke powerfully on suffering and the cost of being a follower of Jesus through the life of Stephen, the first martyr for Christ as recorded in Acts 6 – 8. Another speaker, Ramez Atallah from Egypt, concluded his talk by showing a news report from Egyptian television (subtitled in English). It had been broadcast there in February 2015, shortly after a horrific massacre in Libya in which Egyptian Christian men were murdered for their faith. It showed 21 kidnapped Egyptian Christians in orange jumpsuits, chained and walking in a line to the place where they would be beheaded. When they arrived at the spot, they were ordered to kneel and their ISIS captors, dressed in black, stood behind them.

This video, filmed by ISIS, is believed to be the only video of an actual martyrdom in the 21st century. It was overwhelmingly powerful to see the calm demeanor of these young Christian men who refused to renounce their faith in Christ, and to hear their prayers to the Lord in Arabic seconds before their execution. A man who had been there later reported that as each man was savagely killed, he cried out, "Jesus Christ is Lord!"

Their last words were words of witness.

The news report also included several interviews with the martyrs' parents, wives, and siblings. Each said they were grateful that their loved ones had been faithful to Christ. They said that they had forgiven the murderers and were praying that they would come to know the love of God though Christ. One young widow said, "The first few days were very difficult, but when I saw that report [the very report we had just watched] on television and I saw how brave my husband was, I was so glad that he did not deny Christ before he was beheaded. I know with certainty that he is in heaven, and I know God will be faithful to his promise to care for us—the widows and the orphans who have been left behind."

After the last interview the well-known Egyptian news presenter sat in silence for several seconds and then, looking at the TV camera, he said, "Where does this power come from? How were they able to forgive the very people who killed their loved ones? How is such a thing possible? We have to find out more about this kind of faith. I have never seen anything like this in my life."

Staying salt in this world costs Christians their lives all around the world. It may only cost us, at least for now, a promotion, or our reputation, or perhaps our job and our comforts. That still makes it hard. But it makes it no less necessary—and, when it is hard and we speak anyway, that makes our message all the more compelling. Will people look at us and hear from us, and then say, "We have to find out more about this faith"?

WITNESS IS NOT AN OPTIONAL EXTRA

Alice Greer, along with her husband, Lee, attended one of our evangelism-training conferences in Chicago twenty years ago. I remember her telling me, "I come from a loving church where we do a terrific job of caring for each other. We pray for and bring food to the sick; we visit the shut-ins and those in hospital; we care for the poor in our city. But I have started asking myself, 'Is the primary purpose of my life to buy cream-of-mushroom soup by the case so I can bring casseroles to others? What about those who do not know Christ? How are we to going to reach them?'"

This was the point that the twentieth-century Archbishop of Canterbury William Temple made when he famously said, "The church is the only society that exists for the benefit of those who are not its members." The Bible is clear that the focus of the church must be not only on maintenance but also on mission, and the focus of a church's ministers must be not only on the pastoral care of the congregation but also on equipping its members in evangelism.

There are many good things we can do as God's people. Congregations need pastoring. Programs need volunteers, and plans need actioning. People who are struggling with the brokenness of this world need to see Christ in our care for them. But… is it possible that social justice, while terribly important, has become for many Western Christians the easy default attitude? Acts of mercy remain popular in our culture. Evangelism, however, is now counter-intuitive and politically incorrect. There will always be something easier and more popular to do than share the gospel. But there will never be anything more necessary to do than to share the gospel. Our witness is not an optional extra in our faith—something for the extroverts, the enthusiastic, the professionals, or the missionaries to get on with. I wonder if the verbal aspect of evangelism has to be re-learned as an active choice and a sacrificial commitment. More than ever, we need to have Alice's question ringing in our heads:

"What about those who do not know Christ? How are we going to reach them?"

WITNESS TRULY MATTERS

My brother Bobby and I are—were—"Irish twins": he was born twelve months and two weeks after me. Everyone who knew my brother loved him. He was full of life with a tremendous wit and a huge heart. But he also made some significant mistakes in his adult life and consequently experienced some hard years. We always remained close, and though he admired my faith, he never made it his own.

While Dick and I were living in the UK, one day Bobby phoned, and I could tell instantly that he wasn't his usual ebullient self. I knew he wanted to tell me something, and finally he said, "Oh Becky, I have such regrets about my life."

"Bobby, that's wonderful!" I said. "Because the gospel makes the most sense to people with regrets."

"Yes," he answered, "but when I look at how I have lived my life—and then I look at your life—I feel so ashamed."

"Ok, I grant that your sins have been more colorful than mine!" I replied. "But do you know what we have in common? We are both sinners who desperately need God's forgiveness. That is why Jesus went to the cross. Jesus died for all of us. No one deserves God's grace. But it's there, waiting for you."

"Yes," he said, "but I'd have to do something to prove to God how sorry I am. To show him I am willing to work hard in order to make things right."

"Bob," I told him, "there is absolutely nothing you can do to fix your problem—because God has already done it. All you need to do is tell God you are sorry, acknowledge your sin, accept Christ's offer of grace through his death and resurrection, and ask him to come into your life as Lord."

Because I had shared my faith with Bobby countless times over the years, I was afraid to get my hopes up—yet I sensed that this time was different. As we were about to hang up he said, "Becky, from the bottom of my heart, thank you."

A few weeks later I felt the Lord nudging me to gather my entire family to celebrate Thanksgiving together when we returned back to the US for the holidays—which we did.

On the day everyone arrived, Bobby walked through the door, and I took one look at him and wondered, "What's happened to Bob? He looks different! So peaceful and joyful." But it was such a busy time of hosting that we never had a private moment alone to ask him.

After everyone had left, we discovered that Bob had left something behind, so we phoned him. He drove back, and finally we had a chance to catch up. He told us that he had finally faced the fact that he'd been running from God his whole life. And he said with such joy, "I finally did it. I told Jesus, 'Yes,' and I surrendered my life. Becky, since that moment, you can't imagine all the prayers that he has answered!"

When Bobby left, I turned to Dick and said with uncontainable joy, "For the first time in my life I know my brother belongs to Jesus."

Exactly five days later, Bobby was killed in a car crash.

As I processed my shock and grief, what I came to see was that God, in his love and mercy, and knowing what was going to happen, had nudged me to gather my whole family for Thanksgiving. God alone knew that this would be the last time my family would ever see Bobby alive on earth; and so, in his infinite mercy, he allowed us to know that Bobby had given his life to him.

One week later Dick and I spoke at his funeral. Afterwards a friend of Bobby's had a party to honor his memory at her restaurant. As we walked in, I said to Dick, "Let's make this short, as I am feeling so drained." But one hour later, we hadn't even taken off our coats! Bobby's friends approached us from every direction for just one reason. They wanted to talk about God.

Two sisters told me they had been raised in a joyless, judgmental church and had turned their back on faith. They said, "When Bobby told you that he had regrets, we were expecting you to come down hard in judgment because of the reasons for his regrets. We were stunned when you said that the gospel is for people who have regrets. We were taught that we always had to appear perfect because our dad was the pastor. If what you were saying is really what Christianity is about, then we want to hear more."

A group of Bobby's friends came up to Dick, looking a bit worse for wear. They talked to Dick for a very long time. They asked him if he really believed that Jesus died for our sin and had truly resurrected? Dick said yes, absolutely! They asked question after question. Then one guy, who had been quiet throughout the conversation, said in earnest, "If Jesus truly was God's Son and rose from the dead and is now in heaven, then there is only one question that matters: 'What does Jesus think about us?'"

We didn't sit down for almost two hours. Finally, after I had thanked the woman who hosted the party, I saw a guy at the bar that I'd known in high school. There were ten empty bottles of beer sitting in front of him. He said, "Becky, I need to tell you that we all saw the difference in Bobby. We saw the peace and a new kind of happiness. I'm not a religious man, but what you and Dick said in your eulogies really made sense. I was especially struck by your comment, 'How can we reject something and consider ourselves intelligent people if we've never even read the accounts of Jesus?' So I've decided to take your challenge. Do you have any suggestions for what I should start reading?"

I wrote down a few Christian books on a napkin and then said, "Why don't you start by reading the Gospels?"

"Ok!" he said. "That's exactly what I'll do!"

As Dick and I were walking out the door, he suddenly yelled across the crowded room, "Hey, Becky... What's a Gospel?"

I had dreaded going to the restaurant that night because I was grieving so deeply. But I left it feeling joy and gratitude to God because we had spent hours talking with Bobby's friends, who wanted real answers for real questions and who sensed something was missing in their lives. Not only that, but they had seen a change in Bobby's life and they wanted to know why he had changed. I kept thinking how thrilled Bobby would be to know he had been a witness to his friends in his two short months of walking with Jesus. Bobby died, yet grace won!

My brother's story reveals that God never gives up pursuing and loving us. My brother's funeral reminds us that the gospel of Jesus Christ is what this world so desperately needs. God keeps pursuing people—and we must not give up either, not ever!

There is no question that evangelism is a challenge in today's climate. We will need courage, sensitivity, patience, and endurance, along with faith and the conviction that the truth of the good news of Jesus Christ must be shared out of our love for him and our love for those around us.

No matter how inadequate or hesitant we may feel, Jesus calls every Christian to be his mouthpiece, his hands, and his feet in the spreading of the gospel. We are to join him in the work that he is already doing. We are to depend on him to speak through us as we show with our actions and share with our words his character and his love. Can there be a greater privilege?

The world is changing. It always is. But the world needs the same message today as it did fifty years ago when much of Western society was at least nominally Christian. It needs the same message today as it did twenty centuries ago when the gospel turned the world upside down. The world needs you, and me, to live out the gospel through our lives, our deeds, and our words. And, in God's strength, we can.

So let us celebrate our smallness and walk in the power of the Spirit, because evangelism is rooted in the supernatural power of God! Let us keep learning the truth of the gospel and its profound relevance to everyone we meet, because evangelism is rooted in God's truth! Let us remember that love is the source and the means of reaching others—that nothing can pry open closed or resistant minds and hearts to the gospel more than expressing the love and compassion of Jesus, because evangelism is rooted in Christ's love!

With whatever time God has allotted each one of us, my prayer is that we will strive as never before to be witnesses who are worthy of the One who was and is and is to come, and who came to earth and sacrificed everything for us and for our salvation. Evangelism is still easier than we think and harder than we imagine: it is both exciting and deadly serious. In all that we are, in all that we do, and in all that we say: Stay salt!

EPILOGUE:
A WORD TO
LEADERS

We are living in extraordinary times with significant challenges and tremendous opportunities for the gospel. Christ Jesus calls all of us to be incorporated into his mission to the world and to be bearers of God's good news. We are sent into our battered world to be signs and agents of his blessed kingdom.

The difficulty is that in the West, in reaction to our contemporary culture, many Christians have lost their sense of purpose and evangelistic call. While believers are right to not impose the gospel, they don't seem to want to expose it either! Many shrink from proclaiming the biblical story to even one person, let alone bringing faith into the public arena.

That is why it is crucial for churches, seminaries, and parachurch ministries to maintain a strong sense of gospel mission. Our task as leaders is to help God's people to carry God's ways and God's words into the world. We need to help Christians to know Christ well but also to make him well known!

And therein lies the problem. What are we to do when the common refrain from believers is that sharing the gospel simply "isn't my gift" or "Evangelism is best done by professionals"? How do we respond to the quote I have heard countless times, wrongly associated with Francis of Assisi: that when it comes to witness, we are to "preach the gospel; and when necessary use words"?

To state the obvious, there is a desperate need for local churches to encourage and equip believers in everyday evangelism. In the same way, the need is urgent for seminaries to offer evangelism courses to future church leaders. The challenge for leaders is to understand our cultural context, without emulating the prevailing culture, succumbing to the latest and greatest technique or approach, or wilting before the demands of cultural pressure. We need a holistic approach to evangelism that is biblically faithful, culturally relevant, Spirit-dependent, and relationally authentic. We need to help Christians revel in how Christ's gospel offers not only eternal life but beauty, truth, goodness, and creativity in our personal lives, in our neighborhoods, and throughout the world.

How, then, can churches equip their members and seminaries instruct their aspiring ministers to be effective in evangelism? Here are some principles I have learned over the years that have helped me to equip believers to be, to do, and to share the good news.

FOR THE CHURCH: IT STARTS AT THE TOP

If the senior pastor of a church does not have a vision or commitment to evangelism, it most likely will not happen. A vision for evangelism starts with the pastor(s) and staff before it ever infiltrates the entire church. Whether a church is large or small, the church leaders need to understand how their particular ministry or gifting is connected to their church's involvement, as a church and as individuals, in the Great Commission.

I have great compassion for pastors because they are required to wear so many hats. Most ministers tell me they are not gifted as evangelists nor have they received any specialized help in evangelism at seminary. But church leaders do not have to be gifted evangelists, though they would be wise to get help from those who have specialized in evangelism (and, for larger churches, to have one evangelist and/or apologist on the staff). Pastors simply need to lead by example and occasionally share from the pulpit their recent experiences in sharing faith—both when it goes well and when it does not! Congregations are greatly helped when they see that their pastor is committed to evangelism even amid some fears, and even though they are not always entirely sure how to do it best.

DEVELOP AN EFFECTIVE STRATEGY

By having a "strategy" for evangelism, I do not mean a formulaic or technique-driven approach. We can learn a lot from the book of Acts in how to engage in evangelism. The approach in the early church is as relevant today as it was 2,000 years ago. There were three things that shaped the apostolic approach to evangelism: they proclaimed the gospel (words); they loved and served their community (deeds); and they called people to repent and put their trust in Jesus (invitation). They did this even in the midst of severe persecution. Equally instructive is how they engaged in the verbal aspect of evangelism. It involved three things…

Personal evangelism: In Acts 8 we are told that believers essentially "gossiped" the gospel: they "preached the word everywhere they went" (Acts 8 v 4). Evangelism was not a program but a lifestyle. It was a natural part of their everyday life because they knew that their mission was to be, as Paul would put it a few years later, "Christ's ambassadors, as though God were making his appeal through us" (2 Corinthians 5 v 20).

Small-group evangelism: The early church used their homes for corporate worship, but they also invited into their homes people who needed help in understanding the full gospel (for instance, Acts 18 v 26b). Since hospitality was a significant part of their culture, they most likely shared a meal together as they explained the gospel and answered their guests' questions in a more private setting.

Proclamation evangelism: Acts gives us many examples of believers speaking to larger groups, such as Paul in the Areopagus (Acts 17 v 22-31) or Peter preaching in the temple courts (Acts 3 v 1-26). In other words, they proclaimed and defended the gospel in the public square.

We also must utilize all three approaches: personal, small-group, and proclamation evangelism. I have often seen ministries use only one approach, but it's not enough. When churches engage in all three approaches together, it is powerful.

EQUIPPING IS A NECESSITY

There is no record of the early church holding evangelism-training conferences! Why not? I often heard the late evangelist and Oxford scholar Dr. Michael Green say that their faith was so emboldened by the gospel and the power of the Holy Spirit that it spilled out of them everywhere they went—they understood that Jesus had called them to be salt and light, and they boldly shared the good news of Jesus. They had a holistic approach to witness. Love and service were at the heart of their evangelism.

But in our post-truth, post-Christian West, ordinary Christians do need help. That is why Dick and I have led evangelism conferences around the world, and why we filmed the training and developed it into a seven-session curriculum called *Empowered*. We have found that effective training covers three aspects of evangelism—and they're the same ones as we just saw in the early church in Acts…

Personal evangelism: Since the majority of people who come to faith do so through a personal relationship with a Christian friend or family member, how do we help Christians to gossip the gospel? Christians today need to be equipped with…

- motivation that is biblical and not formulaic
- the mission: understanding that God's call to mission is to every Christian
- the means: how God has given us his supernatural resources, so learning, for example, to lean on the power of the Holy Spirit
- the message: helping believers understand the content of the gospel and how to explain it, defend it, and reveal its relevance
- the model: grasping Jesus' example of witness, so that they follow in his footsteps, evangelizing in the context of relationships in authentic, sensitive, provocative ways

Small-group evangelism: As I have already written, a very effective tool in evangelism is exposing unbelievers to the irresistible person of Jesus. I have found Seeker Studies to be a good place to start with unbelievers, once we have engaged in spiritual conversations and there is some level of trust. Then a follow-up tool should be used, such as the excellent evangelistic courses for small groups like *Christianity Explored* or *Alpha*. Which tool we use depends on where the unbeliever is in his/her spiritual journey. If they are new to exploring faith, then introducing them to Jesus through a Seeker Bible Study, to which a few other unbelievers could also come, is very effective. But if skeptics have more Bible knowledge and seem to be spiritually farther along, then these other tools can be a good place to start.

Proclamation evangelism: This is an important yet often neglected aspect of evangelism, especially in America. The public defense of the gospel is critical. When we use creative and culturally sensitive ways to proclaim the gospel and take questions afterwards, it not only builds the faith of believers but is often used by God to bring unbelievers to faith in Christ.

ONE CHURCH, ONE EXAMPLE

Not long ago Dick and I led an evangelism conference at the historic All Souls Church, Langham Place in London (where the late John Stott was once the rector). We met with the ministerial staff well before the event, and together we developed a strategy.

In early September Hugh Palmer, the rector of All Souls, told the congregation that the focus that fall (being British, he called it "autumn"!) would be on developing a deeper love for Jesus: on falling in love with Jesus all over again—because as that happens, he said, the gospel becomes more alive, we are spiritually refreshed, and we want to give to unbelievers what we have received. He encouraged the church to join a small group that fall and to use the Seeker Study I had written from the gospel of Luke: *Uncovering the Life of Jesus*.

For seven Sundays the ministers preached on the seven passages from that Seeker Study. At the evening service, they then looked at the same passage, but from an apologetic angle. For example, if a story dealt with Jesus doing a miracle, then the evening sermon would address what to say to skeptics who do not believe in the supernatural.

In early November Dick and I gave our evangelism training conference. It was extremely well-attended because the vision and the enthusiasm from the pastoral staff had proved infectious—the conference was advertised as helping non-evangelists, and there was a tremendous foundation of prayer.

At Christmas, the church held their annual Christmas outreach events, and this time Christians felt more confident in inviting their unbelieving friends.

After Christmas the pastors encouraged church members to follow up by starting Seeker Studies with their friends, which many of them were by now familiar with, having heard the passages preached on.

Coupled with lots of prayer, it was a powerful strategy, and we saw encouraging fruit. But it was never intended as a one-off check-box exercise, because it takes time for Christians to develop confidence and competence in sharing their faith. That is why churches need to offer evangelism training every year—along with seminars on apologetics and even a Saturday workshop on leading Seeker Bible studies.

We need to be patient, to persevere, to train regularly, and to lead by example in our own evangelism, doing it all prayerfully. Church leaders show by what they do and say what the priorities of the Christian life are. If evangelism is spoken about and pursued personally and prioritized publicly by the leadership, then over time members catch the vision and start to witness lovingly, authentically, and in dependence upon the Spirit. They discover that they are having good conversations, answering many questions reasonably well, speaking of Christ, and opening up the Bible with friends and neighbors. And then the church begins to see people coming to faith. At that point, the witness of the church becomes self-perpetuating, confidently prayerful, and truly, thrillingly exciting!

BIBLIOGRAPHY

Sam Allberry, *Is God Anti-gay?* (The Good Book Company, 2013)

Ernest Becker, *The Denial of Death* (Free Press, 1973)

Peter L. Berger, *A Rumor of Angels* (Doubleday Anchor, 1970)

G.K. Chesterton, *Chesterton at the Daily News* (Routledge, 2011)

Steve Carter, *This Invitational Life* (David C. Cook, 2015)

Frederick Catherwood, *At the Cutting Edge* (Hodder & Stoughton, 1995)

Richard Dawkins, *The God Delusion* (Bantam Books, 2006)

Marva J. Dawn, *Powers, Weakness, and the Tabernacling of God* (Eerdmans, 2001)

Os Guinness, *Fool's Talk* (IVP USA, 2015)

Os Guinness, *Impossible People* (IVP USA, 2016)

Yuval Noah Harari, *Sapiens* (Harper, 2014)

Carrie Boren Headington, *Acts to Action: The New Testament Guide to Evangelism and Mission*, ed. Susan Brown Snook and Adam Trambley (Foreword Movement, 2018)

Christopher Hitchens, *God Is Not Great: How Religion Poisons Everything* (Twelve Books, 2007)

Christopher Hitchens, *Letters to a Contrarian* (Basic Books, 2009)

Richard F. Lovelace, *Dynamics of Spiritual Life* (IVP USA, 1979)

John Lennox, *Can Science Explain Everything?* (The Good Book Company, 2019)

C.S. Lewis, *Mere Christianity* (HarperCollins, 2015)

C.S. Lewis, *The Last Battle* (First Colliers Books Edition, 1970)

C.S. Lewis, *The Screwtape Letters* (MacMillan Paperbacks Edition, 1961)

Abdu Murray, *Saving Truth* (Zondervan, 2018)

Stephen Neill, *Call to Mission* (Fortress Press, 1970)

Lesslie Newbigin, *The Gospel in a Pluralistic Society* (Eerdmans, 1989)

Kathleen Nielson and Gloria Furman, ed., *Joyfully Spreading the Word* (Crossway, 2018)

Flannery O'Connor, *Mystery and Manners* (Farrar, Straus & Giroux, 1969)

J.I. Packer, *Evangelism and the Sovereignty of God* (IVP USA, 1991)

Blaise Pascal, *Pensees* (Dover Edition, 2003)

Leanne Payne, *The Healing Presence* (Baker, 1995)

Rebecca Manley Pippert, *Discovering the Real Jesus* (The Good Book Company, 2016)

Rebecca Manley Pippert, *Hope Has its Reasons* (IVP USA, 2001)

Rebecca Manley Pippert, *Out of the Saltshaker* (IVP USA, 1999)

Rebecca Manley Pippert, *Uncovering the Life of Jesus* (The Good Book Company, 2015)

Wilhelm Reich, *The Mass Psychology of Fascism* (Farrar, Straus & Giroux, 1970)

Rick Richardson, *You Found Me* (IVP USA, 2019)

Muriel Rukeyser, *Out of Silence: Selected Poems* (Northwestern University Press, 1994)

Fleming Rutledge, *The Crucifixion* (Eerdmans, 2015)

Aleksandr Solzhenitsyn, *The Gulag Archipelago* (Harper & Row, 1976)

John R.W. Stott, *The Cross of Christ* (IVP USA, 1986)

Rico Tice, *Honest Evangelism* (The Good Book Company, 2015)

Miroslav Volf, *Exclusion and Embrace* (Abingdon Press, 1996)

Stephen Westerholm, *Righteousness, Cosmic and Microcosmic* in *Apocalyptic Paul: Cosmos and Anthropos in Romans 5 – 8*, ed. Beverly Roberts Gaventa (Baylor University Press, 2013)

N.T. Wright, *Surprised by Hope* (Harper Collins, 2008)

N.T. Wright, *The Resurrection of the Son of God* (Augsburg Fortress, 2003)

Ravi Zacharias, *The Grand Weaver* (Zondervan, 2007)

ACKNOWLEDGMENTS

There are so many things that go into the writing of a book. *Stay Salt* reflects the fruit of my entire ministry: from my early days of student ministry with InterVarsity Christian Fellowship at Reed College, Willamette and Whitman in the Pacific Northwest, through two decades of church ministry across America, our international ministry around the world and, most recently, our seven years of ministry in Europe. This book represents years of reflection, thinking and reading, endless conversations, and countless talks and lectures addressing many topics but ultimately centered around one thing: how do we present the good news of Jesus? How do we motivate, teach, and train Christians to be witnesses for such a time as this?

I owe so much to tremendous partnerships with extraordinary leaders both at home and abroad where we have ministered side by side: most recently, my friends and colleagues at The Oxford Centre for Christian Apologetics in the UK, whose passion and gifts for presenting the gospel are legendary; along with the late, great evangelist Michael Green. The opportunities to speak not only at the large events but to teach and equip churches and students in holistic evangelism—especially in preparation for outreach missions—have been a deep joy.

I am also grateful for the opportunity to minister to university students across the UK through the ministry of UCCF. To teach personal evangelism and introduce them to Seeker Bible Studies, and then to see the tremendous fruit that resulted as they put into practice what they had learned, was beyond thrilling. I am also indebted to Lindsay Brown's wonderful partnership in the gospel. His ministry, Feuer, which trains and establishes university evangelists in every country of Europe, is inspired and so necessary!

We are so grateful for the guidance, support, and prayers of our friends. I owe a special debt of thanks to: Lady Elizabeth Catherwood, Jim and Ruth Nyquist, Os and Jenny Guinness, David and Pam Bock, Paul and Virginia Friesen, Hugh and Clare Palmer, Stephen and Ruth Shaw, Stephen and Amanda Clark, David and Stephanie Bailey, Greg and Carrie Boren Headington, Thena Ayres, Sherri Divozzo, Tom and Lovelace Howard, and to our beloved Louisville friends Bob and Judy Russell, John and Jane Chilton, John and Elizabeth Hoagland, Jr., Doris Bridgeland, and Austin and Susie Pryor—and to so many more!

Deep gratitude goes to Tim Thornborough, Carl Laferton, and their wonderful colleagues at The Good Book Company. Carl has not only been an endlessly patient, thoughtful, and brilliant editor, but he is truly a friend. And to Robert Wolgemuth, my very wise agent, I thank you.

Most of all I thank my husband Dick, to whom this book is dedicated. He tirelessly read and reread every single page and made critical suggestions and corrections, but it's his unswerving support, loyalty, and love that I cherish most. To have a companion who truly knows and loves the Lord and who is so fully devoted to ministry is a gift from God beyond compare. Thank you to our beloved siblings and my nieces and nephews who prayed for me, and I am especially grateful to our children—Elizabeth, David, Patti, and Tom—and to our precious grandchildren, who encouraged me when I was flagging, and whose prayers I cherish more than they know.

thegoodbook
COMPANY

BIBLICAL | RELEVANT | ACCESSIBLE

At The Good Book Company, we are dedicated to helping Christians and local churches grow. We believe that God's growth process always starts with hearing clearly what he has said to us through his timeless word—the Bible.

Ever since we opened our doors in 1991, we have been striving to produce Bible-based resources that bring glory to God. We have grown to become an international provider of user-friendly resources to the Christian community, with believers of all backgrounds and denominations using our books, Bible studies, devotionals, evangelistic resources, and DVD-based courses.

We want to equip ordinary Christians to live for Christ day by day, and churches to grow in their knowledge of God, their love for one another, and the effectiveness of their outreach.

Call us for a discussion of your needs or visit one of our local websites for more information on the resources and services we provide.

Your friends at The Good Book Company

thegoodbook.com | thegoodbook.co.uk
thegoodbook.com.au | thegoodbook.co.nz
thegoodbook.co.in